Moving Away From Anxiety and Writing Out My Bread Crumb List

By Samantha Glynn

ISBN-13:
979-8742133100
ISBN-10:
8742133100

Book cover artwork by Charlotte Dooley

Acknowledgements

Thanks to my usual book publishing team (Helen and Charlotte) for making this second book in the series possible. You've done a great job again. Thanks also go to my extended family and friends for their encouragement.

Introduction

I had intended to have written this second book a lot sooner than this. Various things had delayed my progress. Last year was a bad health year for me and I had an operation, spending four days in hospital. I then had a diagnosis of Parkinson's to deal with, which was initially a bit of a bombshell but I have come to terms with it now. I had also been busy helping motivate and support my son through his GCSEs. At one point he had 14 exams in two weeks. The amount of content they had to cover seemed ludicrous.

Why had I written my first book? I remember trying to tell everyone about my story of stress and psychosis when I saw them. So I decided it was easier just to get it all down before the memories seemed to fade, although they haven't just yet. I still remember it like it was yesterday. People could then get my book if they wanted to and I wouldn't feel the need to personally tell my story so much. I had messages from friends that had read my book and found it helpful, and this made me happy.

My first book also talked about my struggle working in a school. In this second book I hope to come across as more positive; important changes had been made at work leading to improvements in the behaviour. We could also see that the surroundings were improving. A large new building was being built after the rundown humanities and canteen blocks had been pulled down. Yes, there still were difficult classes and resources were tight but I think after six years I had eventually 'got it' and fitted in. So much so that when redundancy reared its ugly head I was eager to return to a school and help out.

My anxiety was easing but it would never completely go away. At least I could recognise it and address it now. Tiredness was still a problem although lockdown had eased this. The first part of this book looks at how I have been mentally (and physically), and how my coping mechanisms were helping. The second part offers advice from my personal experiences and the third part details the ups and downs of self-publishing. I had looked at writing about anxiety as a hobby but in reality it was so much more than this, as it was therapeutic and I liked the way it provided a record of my experience for others.

Part 1
Moving Forward

So how were things going since I had started living again? Not bad; in fact I considered my mental health as much better although it wasn't perfect. I still get nervous, just like other people do, but sometimes over silly things. Part of the recovery is recognising that worrying is sometimes silly and that it will not actually help. By the end of writing this book my feeling of constant dread had subsided and that was a huge relief.

Notable events since my last book included attending the World Championships in Athletics in London. 'That's strange for someone with anxiety' you may say, considering the sheer number of people attending, but I was so glad we went. I had booked four tickets a year in advance – it was easier that way as I had a year to adjust to the fact I was going and to not worry about it yet. In the end my husband was working so I asked my mum-in-law to go as my 'carer'. Yes, those suffering anxiety needed carers too. Especially when doing something out of their comfort zone.

I'm lucky I have quite a few people I can call upon to accompany me if it is all too much. The athletics worked out well. I couldn't have coped going on my own with my sons. If I did it a second time maybe, but not the first.

The first hurdle (pardon the pun) was to meet my mum-in-law on the train. We got to the station early and I worried whether the taxi had picked her up on time. She sent us a text and it was a relief to find we had got on the right train. Getting on and off the train always came with the stress of 'will that automatic door open?' The journey was good and the people around us seemed to be going to the athletics too. I have since met someone who told me she needed her mum to physically force her onto a train due to her anxiety of them.

Once we got to Stratford International the sheer number of people became obvious. We followed the crowd up the escalators and all the time I was making sure we were together. It was well signposted and we soon could see the stadium. I started to get excited and this feeling wiped away any nerves. We were going to see Usain Bolt! I loved the signature signs he made and hoped to see him do them today.

It took a while to get into the stadium, there were so many gates and we kept getting directed to another one. Finally we went through security and I could see we had made it in time to see all but the first hurdles race. We found our stairs and as we entered the stadium I was amazed and taken aback by all the colours and sounds and the atmosphere. We walked up the extremely steep steps to nearly the top and sat down. A bit of anxiety was probably good as we climbed the stairs as it meant I was careful and didn't tumble back down them.

Sitting down I couldn't take it all in to start with. My eldest son sat next to me. I noticed that he kept checking if his phone was there and I asked if he was alright. Maybe anxiety did get passed on through the generations. He said something about too many people. I pointed out that if there weren't that many people there wouldn't be the atmosphere. It was true, the roar of the crowd was pretty impressive.

We watched the hurdles and the relay events including Usain Bolt who rather disappointedly didn't do his showman moves that much but I could sense his charisma even from such a distance. The big screens helped and we all had a laugh over the Oblivious cam, Bolt cam, Dance cam and Kiss cam which were thankfully based on the other side of the stadium!

It finished with the pole vault. I used to do athletics but

the possibility of injury from the pole vault seemed endless so this was something I never tried.

When we were waiting to leave at the bottom of the stadium my son looked up at the rows of seats that had held us up. 'Is that all that held us up?' he asked. He didn't seem too worried but I was concerned about his way of thinking. I think the phrase is an over-thinker.

I had taken action on many of my ideas to reduce anxiety, notably:

1) Getting a cat

2) Laughing more

… Oh dear and that's about it, but I had tried new things. It was all with mixed success I have to say.

Let's start with the cat. We had a visit from the rescue centre to check if the house was suitable for a cat. I had decluttered as much as possible, my son and I had always been hoarders. I had even cleaned the toilets, not that the cat was likely to use them!

We passed the inspection and a key factor was not being on a main road. Our cat, as far as we know, doesn't go near the road, which is a relief; she stays in our garden and neighbouring ones. Yes we did get a cat.

I remember being nervous about going to the centre to choose one. The first two cats we saw were not ideal, one would swipe out at you all of a sudden and not let you stroke her. The other was way too independent and liked to play but I couldn't see myself picking her up. We were about to leave when the lady remembered she had one called Sherry. So we walked round to her compartment.

I remember Sherry coming down from the upstairs part and rubbing her head against my legs. I reached down and touched her; she was so soft and I think she was purring. We each took it in turns to go in and see her being careful with the double door so she didn't escape. Outside, my husband and I were watching how the kids were with her and we decided she was the one. We couldn't take her home yet as she was due to be spayed.

During our wait for her collection I kept thinking how cold she would be in her outside compartment. We collected her early as they found she had already been spayed. We had to keep her in for a long time to make sure she didn't run off when we let her out. In fact, the first time we let her out I grabbed her before she climbed the fence. I was a self-confessed control freak and would need to learn that cats can't be controlled. She'll feature quite a bit in my recovery.

I had been able to laugh more over that year either at home with the family or out with the girls. A meal at the Toby Carvery just before Christmas had been fun. Again we had taken silly pictures around the table which would appear on Facebook. I'd seen the odd funny film such as *A Bad Moms Christmas* and laughing had made me feel good. 'Make Fun one of your 5-a-day' was on my 'little happy thoughts' calendar.

Lying in bed after Christmas 2018, I had reflected on how little exercise I had done that year. I was now in pain waiting for a hysterectomy so I couldn't see myself doing any for a while. In the future I had briefly planned to do a fun run with my sons; I'm not sure how up for that they were. Once recovered, I could join the gym. I'd been saying that for the past year!

Over the last two weeks I had lost so much blood I was feeling dizzy on my walk into town. I'd worried about some additional tablets I was on. They were Norethisterone and possible side effects were nervousness (great!) and inflammation of veins (after my leg trouble on the way back from Thailand a few years ago this was a worry). But I'd probably have to be on them until my operation.

When I got home my delivery of goji berries and cinnamon bark oil had cheered me up. How had I got into aromatherapy and goji berries? For aromatherapy my original thought was 'is there like a snuff box I could buy to sniff if I got anxious?' My colleague from work had just set up a Facebook page for essential oils and aromatherapy and I arranged to go round to her house to check out some oils.

I took the boys with me and found her place pretty easily. As we walked in the smell was lovely; she had oil for stress diffusing. Between us we sniffed each of the essential oils commenting on their smell. There was only one that I disliked – it smelt like a pet shop. We then tried some goji berry juice and some doughnuts made with orange oil.

At the end she gave me some details and some rollerball bottles so that we could apply some oils. I don't use these much now but they definitely helped me fight some of the remaining anxiety I had felt.

At my latest mental health review I had mentioned that I had used oils and the doctor said that the oils had made me stop rushing around and concentrate on my breathing. 'The olfactory system is the only sensory system that involves the amygdala and the limbic system in its primary processing pathway' and smells can be linked to pleasurable experiences for instance eating a lemon meringue pie. The amygdala plays a big part in anxiety. It may also be a placebo effect. For instance, if you hear that an oil will help with something and then you use it and feel better because of this [18]. Either way, essential oils have helped take the background feeling of anxiety away and I keep my diffuser by my bed. Goji berries seemed to be keeping my cold sores away and that was also good. But things hadn't always been plain sailing.

Our cat Sherry had developed a nasty cough and had sporadic breathing difficulties. She would come in from outside and crouch forward wheezing heavily. We discussed what could be causing it and my oils were blamed. What if she was allergic? I'd have to build my own oil shed outside.

One day she got so bad I phoned the vet helpline. They asked if we had used any new perfumes and my heart sank. We got her to the vets and he gave her some antibiotics and a worming tablet. Within a day she was better and I could use my oils again. I think she had picked up something from when she was in with other cats, in the cattery whilst we were away in France.

Sherry hated other cats. When we had dropped her off at the cattery she had hissed at the other cats next to her and attacked the glass. Even cute kittens were targeted. So the friendly staff put up a screen so she couldn't see them. I even took in anxiety tablets for her once. That is a bit ironic, cat and owner both on anxiety tablets. The cattery would send us photos of Sherry during her stay and she looked relaxed enough. She was clearly glad to see us when we arrived to pick her up though. One time she meowed loudly at my son and then hung spread-eagled on the door so it was hard to open.

My cat may not have helped with my OCD, I now had more to worry about when leaving the house in the morning – especially in the summer; 'What if I shut her out in the conservatory?' she would boil to death. A succulent plant I had left in there whilst away on holiday had suffered such a fate. I would sometimes think 'Had getting a cat been more stressful or actually helped with stress?' One day as I worked on my laptop in bed she jumped on the bed and came over to me nudging and purring letting me stroke her. I realised then she had helped and my oxytocin levels had probably improved. On the first night we let her out of the dining room she had climbed on to my legs in bed and I had gone to sleep with a smile.

Recent mental health training had pointed to another possible way to combat anxiety. This was increasing serotonin levels. Apparently dark chocolate can do this and is said to be good for anxiety. Serotonin is a neurotransmitter that is known to improve mood and positive feelings [2]. I had many of the symptoms of serotonin deficiency. Namely: generalised anxiety, negative thoughts, poor memory and focus (I'm diffusing rosemary oil at the moment to help with that) and agitation. So what could I do about it? Exercise, yes I know I need to fit that in somehow. A much better option for me right now is to eat more dark chocolate! [6]

How was I getting on reducing the amount of caffeine I was consuming? Well I didn't consume any at night mainly because it could keep me awake, but during the day there was no way I was going to reduce it. As I arrived at work a cover supervisor was filling his vape machine thingy ready to face the day and others were already on the coffee. As for beer, I still loved the taste but managed to substitute it sometimes with non-alcoholic beer.

Most days I would have a fuzzy head by the end of the day due to all the stresses. I would start to feel better when leaving work and a beer later would help me reset my mind. My doctor had asked me about my caffeine and alcohol consumption when I had told him about my palpitations. I had been fairly honest. He arranged for me to have an ECG monitor fitted and this coincided with an Ofsted visit to the school. Amazingly I had only had four palpitations that day and all at work of course, and I had pressed the button on the monitor at these times: once walking into work, twice in lessons and once in the corridor. Thankfully the ECG came back as OK.

So how was work going? It seemed to be less manic now and just recently there had been an increase in staff which could only be a good thing. There was even another science tutor at least until Easter which would be great. Before this I had woken up with a feeling of stress and anxiety. For the first time ever I had woken up literally gasping for air. I know this was caused by a performance management meeting I had had that day. At least I had spoken out when I thought some objectives were a little unrealistic. To me even though I did OK each year, performance management seemed like an extra pressure that could be done without and I had seen its sometimes negative effect on teamwork.

I had developed good relationships at work and was talking about a class with their teacher. This class seemed unable to do practical work. Examples of what they would do included burning their (or sir's) pens in the Bunsen burner. Fiddling with crucibles so much that they broke and basically not following instructions. Many a time the practical had to be abandoned. We said, 'What could be done?' I suggested volunteers from the community working with pairs of students. The teacher said, 'What, like outside intervention?' Pondering this I said, 'Might need divine intervention!'

At least our Executive Headteacher seemed to be taking an interest in the school. He had even acknowledged our hard work. He reminded us that our students had very low aspirations due to the deprived area and it was our job to continue praising them and encouraging them. There seemed to be more help with planning lessons now too and some more online resources. I could feel myself becoming more positive and I even coped doing a duty each week out in the quad. Occasionally the kids would need reminding to get off the tabletops or the tempting catering trolley next to the kiosk or to generally leave each other alone. But the main hazard it seemed now was the incoming seagulls diving for scraps of food. The lady who I shared duty with had had some seagull mess hit her on her bare foot as it was now sandal weather.

I still had bouts of anxiety but they weren't as common. One morning my son had an IT exam so I was on edge about this. It wasn't helped that on the way in there were roadworks and traffic lights and I nearly had to squeeze the car between a bus and some cones. In the end I gave up and the bus came out anyway. My heart rate had gone up but I managed to control it.

Once in work my son phoned and I started to panic that he had not made it into school and that he would miss his exam. It was about his orthodontist appointment that wasn't until Thursday. I didn't really relax until his exam was over at 11.30, not that I could do anything about it. He would have most of his exams the next year so what sort of gibbering wreck would I be by then? What was my anxiety level like now?

It was time to take the anxiety test that I took for my last book. So I went back to www.recoveryformula.com [15] and the results are in.

'Your level of affectedness by anxiety and panic is not severe but strong enough to affect your life and your person on a regular basis. You tend to let things get to you. You are an over-reactor and you're probably very emotional. You're sensitive and take things personally. You're a worrier and a "what-if" thinker. You might have a hard time being assertive, especially with certain people. You probably don't manage stress well'.

My numerical value was 53%. It was 60% when I wrote my first book so I am moving in the right direction. But there is clearly some work to be done.

Reading the above it is all true. I still had moderate anxiety. But how much of this could I actually change? A couple of questions in the quiz had stuck out as maybe raising my percentage above 50%. These were 'I experience twitching, trembling or shaky feelings'. I had put strongly agree for this as my Parkinson's makes this quite bad. 'To me the world is a scary place'. I think a lot of people would strongly agree with this at the moment (especially if they watch the news on a regular basis).

The quiz also asked about dreams. I was still experiencing vivid dreams and I had a recurring one about packing. Normally in the dream this was left to the last minute when returning from holiday. I never seemed to get it done on time. Looking at websites this signifies change. Work was going to change for me in September. I would be based in my room and joined by students who had been removed from lessons (parked). This did seem on the face of it a hard job and I would have to see how it went. Not too well, as you will see further on.

It is true that sometimes you have to face your fears. Before Christmas two years ago we were due to meet my sister in Bognor Regis to exchange presents and catch up. I had a long-standing fear of using the big car but agreed to take Mum and Dad and the boys down there in it. I would lie in bed worrying about it, my heart pounding. However, I managed to keep a positive attitude and picked them up from Deal after sorting the fan out so I could clear the mist that formed on the windscreen. Luckily we had a lot of boot space as there was a lot to take. Near their house the roads are very narrow and I had to have a second attempt at turning left as another car had only just let us through. I had learned to take it slowly and have another go if necessary after scuffing the car outside my mum-in-law's house. The journey wasn't too bad and it was good to have Mum and Dad as back-up in case we got lost or the car broke down. I still don't use the bigger car regularly but I knew I could if I had to.

I have made two significant journeys on my own since this, once to my sister's and once to a campsite in Sussex, to meet some friends. There were so many things to worry about on a long journey now. Here are the things I worry about and how I try to overcome them:

1) Speed cameras. There are so many different types of speed cameras now. Average speed cameras, cameras in vans, the usual ones and ones on motorway bridges. I just assured myself that I'm a slow driver and the satnav would give me the speed limits when I didn't know them because the road signs were few and far between.

2) The car would breakdown. My little Toyota Yaris hadn't let me down yet but it was getting older at over 10 years old. I assured myself I had RAC cover and again the satnav would help giving them our location.

3) Would there be enough service stations? I would make sure I had enough food and drink and always had more than half a tank of fuel for long journeys.

4) My right leg might cramp up at some point, making driving difficult and painful. It had done this a few times but only when we were nearly home. My circulation in my right leg wasn't great. I told myself I would pull over and take a break if necessary.

5) Debris in the road. This is a recent worry. We had been coming back from a morning in Faversham away from the crowds at Huckleberry Woods. We were doing about 65

on an A road when I noticed a folding camping table with one of its legs up in our lane. I quickly checked my mirrors and there was no one in the other lane so I quickly moved out. We were lucky and I'm glad I had quick reactions. As we drove by the next layby people had stopped and were on their phones. On the other side of the road we could see a police car making its way there to remove the table.

6) Not getting enough sleep before driving. This was particularly a worry if we were staying somewhere else. Getting to sleep had been better lately as I was usually knackered. So I had recently ditched my old out-of-date sleeping pills, I had used when training to teach and whilst working at Pfizer after my children came along. I now take my lavender pillows and try not to worry about the journey until the morning.

There are probably more things to worry about than that. But everyone has their own fears, or are there people out there with no journey worries at all? I'd recently managed to drive on my own to a health centre nestled in an unknown area of Ashford for my neuropsychologist meeting. There were just so many roundabouts but my satnav got me to within 300m.

I arrived early and luckily took my own drink and snack seeing as it was nowhere near any shops. The meeting went well. I even managed to mention my first book which she recorded in my notes. She said she wondered what psychosis was like and we agreed she probably couldn't do her job if she had experienced it. Still, maybe my book would be an insight. She wrote in her medical review 'Mrs Glynn presented appropriately dressed and well kempt (I guess I had brushed my hair and was no longer wearing my husband's shoes!). She engaged well and maintained good eye contact throughout the assessment (I do sometimes like being the centre of attention). Her speech was spontaneous with normal rate, tone and volume. She described her mood as "happy" (probably because I'd achieved something by getting to the appointment). I did pretty well on the memory test too. I got 98% although I didn't quite understand her pronunciation of President of the United States!

I was also pleased that I had got the boys involved in things outside school. Since getting the cat the eldest hadn't been able to do air rifle in the garden in case she got shot, so I took him and his friend to a shooting club. You may think it is weird that someone with anxiety would take their son shooting but I actually find it relaxing. The only time I got a bit worried about it all was once when they didn't wipe their hands before eating after shooting. I had looked it all up on Google and apparently traces of lead could be ingested with food after handling lead pellets. I then read on about breathing in lead after the shot was fired. In my head I could visualise the plumes of lead-containing smoke. I managed to snap out of it. After all, the range was well ventilated and we would make sure hands were wiped in the future. It was important that they had a hobby and everything came with a risk of some sort.

My other son liked football so we would meet his friend at a park so they could have a kick about. I would sit in the car reading a book as it wasn't the best of areas. People would walk by and I'd subconsciously check out their threat level! I knew I was a bit of a control freak at times. Once some young adults and other kids were using the other goal and I wondered how this would pan out. In the end they all started playing together and no harm was done.

One weekend I'd been unable to take either of them – I couldn't drive when I was light-headed. My physical illness had started on Friday at work. My revision class with a small group had gone well in the morning looking at lungs and breathing. However, first period the other tutor and I were given the task of taming a class for a practical. They had not had a regular teacher for a while as the NQT had left before Christmas. I knew a few of the students but from a while back. Within 10 minutes we realised we wouldn't get the entire practical done. The effort from this lesson had wiped me out and by the time it came to supporting in another lesson my vision had started to go around the edges. I knew that this wasn't right and told the teacher I had to leave. I rested up in the staffroom until I felt safe enough to drive home. I realised on the phone to the nurse that my breathing had become laboured. I had an explanation later from the doctors as my iron level had dropped drastically and I lacked haemoglobin. Some iron pills gradually got me back to tickety-boo and my blood pressure eventually increased from a low level. Anxiety in itself can cause low blood pressure and mine had been very low [3].

The table that follows compares my recent experience of physical and mental illness:

Physical illness	Mental illness
Could be scary	Could be scary
Could be quantified (e.g. an iron serum level of 2.5 μmol/L). You also get a diagnosis.	Was harder to quantify in a form employers could take note of. I guess you could get a diagnosis (e.g. suffers anxiety).
Could make you tired.	Could make you tired
Can make your brain fuzzy and dozy.	Can make your brain fuzzy and dozy.
Could affect your confidence.	Could affect your confidence.
Sometimes hard to talk about.	Getting easier to talk about.

There are quite a few similarities between the two. I'm lucky at work I could be honest about my illness. Though I'm not sure which was more awkward, talking about women's trouble or anxiety. After Christmas while getting my coffee I had explained that I had needed a blood test. The maths tutor, a man, had asked why. I had explained women's trouble and I had lost so much blood (maybe I am a little too honest at times). He had lost concentration and overfilled his kettle. Talking about anxiety in the staffroom was OK. Occasionally a cover teacher would say he had been anxious. It was always easier to talk about it when someone else brought it up.

Whilst off sick I woke up from another nap and I could hear the wind howling outside. I had dreamed during my naps which was a bit weird as I couldn't have been asleep long. I saw my sister and Dad in my dream mending cars. Then my dad got ill and I had to get him to sit down. To dream of fixing your car represents your attempt to get back on track in your life (dreambible.com). I had chosen to remain out of the rat race for another day. Palpitations maybe caused by my low blood pressure had reminded me this was a good thing. But as I contemplated going back to work I imagined myself being able to lock myself in a room and putting a do not disturb sign up. Could I go in in my dressing gown?

My return-to-work interview would surely be soon as I

had missed the last one as I had got sick again. Returning tomorrow 'Would I be able to sit down and eat when I became light-headed?' Just as I was pondering this a delivery arrived that cheered me up (business cards for my writing, see Part 3) and a bag for my Tibetan singing bowl. I had got the Tibetan singing bowl to help me meditate or get some relaxation. It was smaller than I expected but I enjoyed using it. The sound it makes is like the sound you get from rubbing the rim of a wine glass (my mum-in-law had suggested just doing that). The tones of the singing bowl seemed to tune in with the mind once I had mastered it. Apparently they confuse cats but Sherry seemed to enjoy it.

I had walked round the Co-op light-headed and looked at the alcohol and walked past despite the medicinal properties of Guinness in regard to iron that people had reminded me of on Facebook. I didn't think it was a good idea as already I felt a bit tipsy even without a drink. In fact I had cut down on alcohol consumption and was starting to try to develop a taste for non-alcoholic beer. There was a new feeling of freedom that came from not relying on alcohol so much.

More recently when my iron levels had recovered we had walked over seven miles and had lunch halfway in a pub. My main reason for walking was the exercise rather than the beer. I had noticed when out walking sometimes when I looked at the floor I imagined falling towards it and making contact with the hard ground. Even walking held its dangers.

When my husband had been in hospital someone in his ward had fallen and hit his head and died. The curtains had been pulled around his body when I arrived to collect my husband. As you can imagine we were quite desperate to get home after this and the nurse discharged him soon after, when the man's naturally distraught daughter came to see her dad.

Other sources of anxiety were walking across a motorway via a footpath, the railings seemed far too low and I managed to keep my eyes forward trying to ignore the deafening sound of the traffic below. We had also walked through some fields on our walk and discussed how in the future they would be built on. This saddened me as the roads were already chaotic around here and it would only add to the stress on the people in the area.

That summer we had had a relaxing holiday – mainly because I took the decision to do what we wanted to do not what others wanted us to do. I had a theory that sometimes it was good to be lazy and stay in your comfort zone as this gave your Amygdala the rest it needed. 'The human brain wasn't designed to pay attention and be alert for hours at a time'. [17] This site also has advice to step out of hectic routines.

I have recently started to read up on mindfulness. It was Ruby Wax that introduced me to this in her book *Frazzled*. It made a lot of sense to take moments to use your senses to appreciate your surroundings and to recognise negative thoughts. Recent counselling at work had also helped.

A lady from Place2be had started to help students at school. She had offered to help me after I had talked about stress in the staffroom. In the end I only needed two sessions to start feeling better. During our sessions we talked about how my job had changed and how I was coping. We also looked at how breathing exercises can help. I needed to say to myself 'I am in control of me' and 'I trust my decisions'. During the breathing exercises I would imagine a safe happy place. I came up with my lounge with my family of four sitting and relaxing watching a movie with the cat relaxing too. This was when I was at my happiest. I also had to imagine being at work when things were going right which they did sometimes, it is worth noting. I would be standing in front of my board talking confidently with the students listening and engaging. If rules were broken I would calmly use the warning system to great effect.

After some quite severe palpitations I was back at the doctors. It had been more like a fluttering that had occurred after having a particularly challenging pair of students parked in my room. In fact I had learned to dread many students being sent out of science lessons to my room due to bad behaviour as their behaviour often continued or escalated in my small room. Sometimes another teacher helped me out and we would have quite a good 'Good cop bad cop routine' going. He had much more authority than I did. We had to be nice enough to encourage them to stay in the room (where else would they go?) and to get them to do some work, and tough enough to get them to realise the seriousness of the situation.

One morning I stood in the kitchen literally wanting to cry with the thought of what I could face that day. The doctor insisted this time that I try to come off caffeine to reduce my palpitations. I did so and fairly quickly the palpitations got better. Now instead of coffee I would have a hot chocolate in the staffroom. It didn't bother me in the end as I felt less tired surprisingly and fewer palpitations reduced my anxiety. I wasn't jittery anymore and a work colleague had noticed this. Caffeine had contributed to my breakdown (see my first book) so it was good to leave it behind. I had recently had the feelings of dread that I had had before my breakdown. Luckily I had got myself out for the day with my mum and younger son and the feelings had passed. It is sometimes hard to get out when you have anxiety as you imagine all the bad things that might happen and you get stuck in a vicious cycle.

Thankfully after about six months there had been a pleasant shift from blaming the teacher to respecting the teacher which would hopefully filter down to more of the students. The staff had been thanked personally in Christmas cards and received gifts from the senior leadership team. There had been assemblies about how teachers were human beings and should be treated as such and they did not come in to be stressed out. A stricter system for behaviour had been introduced where students would be given warnings up to a C4 and then sent to the hall for time-out. If they did not conform they may be isolated in another school which should be a good deterrent. It was early days but the early signs were good and things were better. There was a new move to staff wellbeing in school and the Head had backed this up with wellbeing weeks where staff could leave earlier than usual and could take part in activities such as yoga in high heels! I particularly looked forward to the bacon butties at briefing on these weeks.

Schools were at breaking points with budgets and poor staff retention. It was hard not to feel the strain when working in them. At least I wouldn't have students parked in my room anymore. They would now be parked for all subjects in the hall with senior management.

Work had been quite good lately although I still dreaded having to do cover. Cover was now shared between the teachers, cover supervisors and tutors, which meant that the instability of external supply teachers had been lost.

Exam season had finished. I found work particularly hard last year as my son was also in year 11. Where I did duty at lunchtime was right opposite the exam noticeboard and there would be a countdown to when the exams started to be posted on this. I was also doing invigilation in the hall and would worry about how my son was doing. We had done a lot of work at home and he had coped very well in the end.

My new head of department had started about a year ago and she worked well with the Head to overcome many of the problems that I had described in my first book. My performance targets seemed more realistic and each staff member had been asked their views on the school in small meetings (I had taken notes to mine). I had been asked to do some sixth form lessons when I had recovered from my operation. Maybe this was a way of getting back into teaching with older students, ones that generally knew how to behave.

Before new behaviour policies had been introduced a supply teacher had complained of his lesson being invaded seven times. Now there was an expectation that could be policed, that students were either in class or in the hall. There were still difficult classes but in general things were getting better. I was conscious that I wasn't working at full cylinders all the time anymore. This was a self-protection policy. You could liken it to physical health. After all if you vomit after eating a particular meal you will avoid this food for a while. If you have a car crash you may avoid doing that manoeuvre or taking that road again. Overwork had made me seriously ill so I was avoiding it. Physical and mental health seemed to become more linked the more I thought about it.

I still had anxiety with everyday things, for example our finances. I had improved since just after my breakdown. I now had online access to my accounts and even had a PayPal account. Recently I had been able to pay off a relatively large loan. I had sat there entering all the numbers and double-checking again and again before pressing the big red button. Our money then seemed to go in the ether where it wasn't in our account and wasn't with the loan company either. Why did this always happen on a bank holiday too? My OCD was rearing its ugly head again. I would be checking sort codes and account numbers until my brain couldn't do it anymore. I definitely couldn't work in banking or accounts.

In a way it was good that I had online banking. If I had done the payment through a branch I may have wanted to check the numbers afterwards and got even more anxious. I had come a long way; before, I would avoid doing transactions online. However, I still had my bag round my shoulder when at work and out and about and checked my wallet before bed. I would also regularly check my house and car before leaving it.

When parking at work I did several checks before leaving my car and had even gone back out to it a couple of times. Was there a skip nearby? Necessitating a huge skip lorry getting near my car? Was I parked too near a driveway? Were my tyres touching and rubbing the kerb? Residents were clearly a bit annoyed about work cars and a couple of times I had been boxed in. Once a red Mercedes was close to my bumper with another car close behind. Luckily I had got out

OK as builders were watching nearby. My heart rate had gone up and I had coped OK. Essential oil roll-ons such as one called Tranquil were also useful for situations like these. It would remind you to breathe in.

I had learned to hold onto positive things and my friend had asked me to send her my positive thoughts of the day. I found this really helped me and I would use messenger to send her messages. It was particularly important on work days when things didn't always go to plan. Here are some of my positive messages.

"Wow only just sat down. Busy day, then I had tutoring to do, then sorting the house and shopping (text speak). Got called Baby Girl at the Co Op xx"

"Felt tired today. But good day really (text speak). Had nice long chat with my boss xx"

"Good day today in with our old department for a while"

She would always reply quickly and it was good. I had been sad when she left work and this was a good way to keep in touch. It was great when she replied with some of her positive points. For instance she would message about learning to drive and her cute niece being born. It was not until you started to document these positive things and thoughts that you would store it in your mind.

If philosophy is a way of thinking, I think it can have a role in combatting anxiety. The next part of this book looks at some of the things I have learned over the years with a hint of philosophy and how I can pass this on.

Part 2
Bread Crumb List

'Bread Crumb List?' I hear you ask. Well I was going to call it the 'Banana Skin List' as it was going to be a list of slip-ups I've made and ways to avoid them for my sons to read. It was particularly apt as I had fallen over twice in recent years. Once, if you remember, was when I fell forwards on slippery rocks at the waterfall in Thailand and the other, I didn't mention, when I fell backwards at work on equally slippery steps.

It had been raining and my shoes were new. I remember being in a bit of a rush to get into work (I'm not sure why, looking back). I felt myself go but I couldn't do much about it. It all seemed to happen in slow motion. I fell hard on my backside and luckily my shoulder bag with my laptop in it took the brunt of the fall. The receptionist, a parent and cover manager were among those that saw me and asked me if I was OK. I got up and managed to get through the day. There was no sharp pain in my back which was a good sign.

I was glad to get to my car after work. But I soon found out my key would no longer work, it had been bent in the fall. Luckily my husband came in to bring the spare key so I could get home and inspect my rather large bruise on my right buttock. I decided to take a picture of it for evidence, in case I would need to make an injury claim later on. I had also broken my laptop in the fall and the keyboard had been replaced at work. If only someone had told me those steps got really slippery; I avoid them now.

I started to think of a long list I could write with similar warnings; everyone's would be different and give advice on possible dangers. But I thought rather than being negative

I'd do a kind of legacy list with positive as well as negative things. It would describe some of my life's events and the advice that would come from these.

Bread crumb trails originated in *Hansel and Gretel* for them to find their way back again but they can also be used for people to follow, and this is their intended use here. What if a bird or outside factor like wind moves them? Well, I'll have to take that risk. It hadn't been successful in the original version of the story but I had to try. Writing this second book has helped me as my nervous breakdown had evolved a conspiracy theory about the safety of my kids. Although they are much older now and I was starting to learn that I couldn't prepare them for everything but I still had a role in helping them through life.

We, my family, had been lost in the woods a couple of times. As a group though, so we could reassure ourselves by saying things like: 'If we keep walking we'll reach the road', 'We can ask someone the way out', 'I have a phone signal', 'I have a good sense of direction', 'We have some drink and food'. All of these are flawed in some way but they did make you feel better. Luckily it is not like Canada, in the UK the forests are not that big.

My list starts quite early on…

Don't assume everyone is as kind as you. I learned this fairly early on at a playgroup. I still remember the playgroup, it was in a modern church with a tall triangular spire. Inside was really large with lots of toys and things to play on. I saw a boy in the middle of the room and said 'you look nice' he just looked at me and said 'go away'. That was a pretty crushing thing to happen to a girl of about six or seven. It's funny what clear memories you can have looking back.

Don't believe everything people say. This relates to one of my operations that I had on my eye squint when I was about five. There are four clear memories about the whole thing. The first memory was of spilling Rice Krispies on my dressing gown in my hospital room. The next was of getting a toy train after the whole procedure and another memory was of having to leave Dad while I got taken in a lift by hospital staff. The fourth and main memory for which this anecdote relates was lying on the hospital bed with a gas mask coming down to my face. I think that's how people were anaesthetised back then. I remember as the mask came towards me I shouted for Mum and waved my arms around. I can still remember how the room looked and the brown mask which was going to form a seal around my face. Again I said, 'Where's Mum?' They said she had gone shopping! I told Mum about this years later and she said she had been told to go by the hospital staff and wasn't allowed to stay. It was done differently then. She most definitely didn't go shopping.

When you feel like coughing you might actually be sick. Again when young I remember getting up from bed and going to the bannisters in the upstairs hall. I looked down and said 'I'm going to cough'. Dad was in the hall downstairs and as I said it I started to vomit and I think some of it hit him on his bald head. My sister had come out to join me and my dad said 'Get her into the toilet and keep her there'. So I was shut in the toilet until I had stopped being sick.

Stick with the subjects you are good at. I'm not sure when I first became interested in science but I remember being given a chemistry kit. I would use it in the family shed and a friend up the road had shown me how to make sparks. I must have been pretty into it all, as I remember crying when one of the test tubes broke. You also need to enjoy the subject as it's probably the one you will do in later life as a job. Even now 30 years on I have to dig out my certificates to scan or show people, you'd think it would be on a database somewhere.

Have your favourite memories of loved ones to hand. For example I had a fond memory of skipping down the road with one of my grandmothers. I also had a memory of a Christmas dinner with my other grandmother when we had a laugh by putting the candles out with turkey drumsticks of all things. It helps you concentrate on your memories rather than the loss when you are parted.

If someone takes the micky out of you being skinny beat them at athletics. There was a gang of popular kids at our school. A couple of them were fairly bulky. They would poke fun at how skinny my sister and I were. Luckily when I was at school there was a five star athletics scheme. I remember I was good at the 800m and would almost lap them doing this. It made me feel better about myself.

The best revenge is doing well. This can apply to any sort of bullying you may experience. I think working hard and getting good GCSEs was a turning point for me and my sister. It meant we could move schools and out of a negative situation. It had got so bad that we couldn't even face going to school to pick up the results. We waited for them to arrive by post, nearly knocking each other over in our race to the front door. Even when it came to collecting the certificates we didn't go in. To us we had done really well in the circumstances and a lot better than our adversaries. It can apply in more situations, for example if you want to get back at an ex. But don't let it become too important. Your happiness is the best thing and the best revenge.

If you have a bad feeling about a change you may be wrong. I remember that my sister and I had applied for a place at grammar school for sixth form. We had got the grades to get in. The morning we were due to go in I said to my sister 'I think this is a bad idea' but in the end it was one of our best decisions. I was probably a bit apprehensive as our bullies at our old school had said 'We know a girl there and we'll make sure no one likes you' or words to that effect. Of course the girls at the new school were able to make up their own minds and we soon had a large circle of friends. We still keep in contact with them now.

Give things a go especially if your friends are there to help. This particularly relates to a canoe trip at university where I braved a slalom course on a fast-running river. I knew I'd be rubbish and had gone on the trip for the social side really. In the end I made it through one gate and just about managed to break out at the river's edge under the instruction of my friends at the riverside who grabbed my canoe.

I was glad to have not swallowed any water as someone I knew had been to the toilet over the bridge as a bit of a laugh. It brought a whole new meaning to logging. But seriously who knows where I would have ended up if I had not managed to 'park' the canoe. Having said that I'm glad I had a friend at uni who encouraged me to get out and do things.

I remember her encouraging me when we were out on what ended up to be a five-hour canoe session in Pembrokeshire. We had stayed near the coast and even saw some seals, but at one point I was drifting out and she gave me a pep talk and some chocolate. I think I crawled out of the canoe when I finally reached our beach. You have got to appreciate the people that are good for your mental health.

Enjoy doing silly things every now and again. During my second year at university I had gone to a toga party. We had walked to it wearing a toga and headband. On the way back we crossed a park area just below the arts building. For some reason we started to roll down the hill. I can still remember it now. Starting off by a tree I rolled on and on, the sky spinning between the green of the grass. I remember becoming worried about taking my sheets for the weekly collection for washing, as they had got covered in grass stains. Looking back I'm really glad I did things like this before I became my anxious self. I might have told myself not to do it as I could break my neck or something. Basically let your inner child out now and again.

Don't judge someone by their hair cut. Apparently I had not been all that interested in my husband when one of his friends came over to tell me that he liked me. I had seen he had a shaved head and thought he's not really my type. Then a few months later he had grown his hair. I think it was in the 90s 'curtain' style. One Friday night I had been round a friend's house and we had had some rather lethal punch before going out. I remember walking down the hill where my house was in a somewhat drunken fashion as a big gang of girls. We arrived at the student union and joined the big queue to get in. There he was in his nice red shirt.

Apparently I said something to the effect of 'I really need the toilet'. Romantic, I know. At which point we went our separate ways and met up later next to the dance floor. He walked me home that night. I remember sitting and watching telly with him for a while. He was criticising the programmes and adverts. He is still fussy about what he watches 26 years later! He then went back to his house and arranged to pick me up the next night for dinner. When he came to the door I was pleased with how he looked as I wasn't too sure, after all that punch I had drunk the night before. We went back to his place and what a result – he was a great cook. He cooked me chicken in a cream sauce and I ate it all. It made a great change from the plain burger, plain pasta and broccoli I used to cook for myself as a balanced diet! I ask myself now, 'What if he hadn't grown his hair?' and 'What if I hadn't drunk that punch?' Things would have turned out so different.

Look out for the pitfalls of a summer ball. People can get carried away at big celebrations. The University Summer Ball was an example of this. I remember walking through the hall halfway through the night and seeing one of my housemates in an ambulance chair. He had overdone it with alcohol. There is a fine line to be found with alcohol; stop at that point before its toxicity and depressant nature takes over. The summer ball is often an all-night affair. I had been so tired after the summer ball once, even though I had taken Pro Plus (please do not take any tablets at a party, even if it is Pro Plus!). I was too tired to pack and kept falling asleep all the way home the next day with my mum.

There is no such thing as being specially selected by post, email, in person or by phone! If it sounds too good to be true it probably is! Also, watch out for those emails you get that say your account is going to be charged or blocked, for example. They are just after your bank details or passwords. Phone the proper company if you are unsure. With scams it is actually helpful to be a little paranoid. Scammers would pick on your weaknesses, for example your desperation to buy a puppy as I saw on the TV recently. Their techniques are becoming increasingly sophisticated. It is always best to handle finances when you are not tired and distracted and check out websites thoroughly. I had recently ordered something online and then afterwards checked the reviews of the website. This is the wrong order to do such things and increased my anxiety levels.

Instructions you have been given may not be clear enough. The best example of this was when I nearly blew up a work building when disposing of waste. Quality Operations had recently moved to a new building but there were lots of chemicals to dispose of in the old building. I and another member of the team were sent to the old lab to get rid of chemicals. We were always told that non halogenated waste should go in one solvent container for disposal and halogenated waste should go in a separate container. So we dutifully separated the chemicals into these categories and started to dispose of them. Suddenly a container which we had placed on a trolley had started to crackle. My quick thinking colleague put it in the fume cupboard and opened the lid. It still continued to crackle as pressure built up with the reaction. We called for help and someone from another lab came in and we had to evacuate. Site team then dealt with the situation and the gas that had been produced. I think if the lid hadn't been open a small explosion may have happened.

We were of course debriefed and they asked what we had put in the container. I said that I remembered putting toluene and nitric acid in the container. My senior manager said that these were the ingredients of TNT! Clearly I needed to do more chemistry with the Open University! And so I did. We didn't really get in trouble and it showed that normal procedures had to be adapted in certain circumstances. The acid should have been disposed of separately in small amounts with water.

Gossip is not power although knowledge can be. This comes with maturity. I used to think that being part of a popular group meant that you needed to gossip about others to be accepted. This is so wrong. You may find things out about other people but you should not share them willy-nilly. Knowledge about others can be important for you and should only be shared if someone is in danger. For example if someone is behaving strangely they may need help. But if 'so and so' danced with someone on a work night out that was up to them.

You may feel inferior if you are with someone who has a well-paid job. Don't be! Organising the house and kids, if you have them, is just as important. Many of the most successful people had great people supporting them at home.

Believe your friends if they say you are too drunk and you should go home! I have some good memories of the hockey tours in Worthing. However, there were times when danger could have ensued and I don't just mean from a hockey stick or a hard hockey ball. One night I had not been able to keep up with the drinking and was the worse for wear at the restaurant. The others were going to go clubbing at a club on the pier after the meal, but they said I should go back to the hotel. Luckily two of them escorted me back to my room. One even took my boots off for me. If they had let me go to the club I might have fallen off the side or something as you could get out onto the pier from the club. I had crossed the fine line I mentioned earlier and I could feel the toxins the next day.

Don't believe your husband if he says it won't hurt if you fall off a bike. I remember one Saturday I had been finishing a hanging basket and my husband had come back from work announcing that we were going out on our bikes.

So he put the bikes on the car and we headed off to Blean Woods near Canterbury. It was June 1999 and my first trip out mountain biking. The ride started off OK and we went through a wooded area watching out for low branches. Then we reached a gravel track and I started to speed up down the hill. I remember thinking I was going to fast (32mph) and so I used the brakes. The bike started to snake and there was little I could do so I unclipped my cycling shoes and waited for the inevitable. With a crash I was down. My husband had come back to see where I was and he realised how bad it was and went to get help. I couldn't even get up when the ambulance arrived and they had to use a sling. Four nights in hospital and a five-hour operation on my elbow followed. My helmet had got hit and I'm pleased my sons use theirs when out cycling.

Don't always go by first impressions. I remember the first time when I met one of my friends just before the birth of my first son. At that moment I thought she was aloof and probably not my type of person. I was wrong and over time we became close friends. I feel at ease in her company and we regularly have 'Swan' nights at a pub near us called The Swan with each other and another close friend. It's great that our sons are good friends too. We are such good friends that even though someone from work thought she was my daughter I still like her. That reminds me, I must put my face cream on.

Be careful what you wish for. I remember saying to my friends once that I had wanted a September baby when I found out my second son was due in November. It turned out that he was born eight weeks early and was a September baby! Being born early is always a risk and we are lucky he is with us now. I still feel guilty about wanting a September baby.

Don't assume your child has followed you when stopped in the high street. This was a scary moment. I had finished getting my money out of a cash machine in the high street and started to walk between the market place to get to the café. My youngest must have been daydreaming as I couldn't see him when we got to the café. My heart jumped and we quickly returned to the cash point. It was a huge relief as he was still there. He was getting anxious and still talks about it now. I'm normally really good at checking they are with me even to the point of checking they are both in the back of the car, after hearing that a family had left one of their children at a service station in France.

Listen to your kids in the back of the car. We were on our way to Birmingham to see my sister and family. We had left a bit late and so we didn't get to the outskirts of Birmingham until about 10pm. The satnav had taken us on a back route I had been on before, which had had a road closed sign once so I had to turn back. This time there was no sign but as we turned right we were faced with a puddle that spanned the road. It was getting dark so we couldn't really see where it ended. My hubby turned to me and said, 'Do you want to do this or shall I, as I've done it more'. I said, 'No it's fine I'll have a go,' taking up the challenge. My boys say they had said not to in the back, but I hadn't heard them at this point. I headed off on a mission to prove I could get through a ford not realising the full extent of it. I kept the revs going and was enjoying the first bit (like off-roading on *Top Gear*!).

My hubby was encouraging me saying to keep the bow wave going but he started to look worried and looked from left to right. We nearly got to the end but the road dipped down and I panicked a bit, the car stopped and within seconds water was coming in. We quickly lifted up all our electrical things like phones and Nintendo DS consoles. There was a cry from the back and we got out of the car and lifted the boys out taking them to a dry part of the road which was only a few feet away. I remember the water being deep enough to wet the top of my trousers.

We looked back at the car and saw it stranded thinking we've done it now. Luckily a group of people drove up in their 4-by-4 and offered us a tow out. My hubby went back in and managed to get the tow rope attached. They pulled it out with relative ease and we watched as it drained out. It was now dark and we were getting cold. I had managed to phone the RAC and my sister with my hand shaking. We weren't far from my sister's so she sent out her hubby to come and rescue the boys. We tried to start the car but it wasn't running right and the electrics had gone weird. The driver's window kept going up and down randomly. We sat in the car and the rescue truck got to us fairly quickly. Apparently he was in the bath when he got called out as the other truck was on another job. We got to my sister's after midnight and gratefully gave our rescuer a bottle of wine from the back of the car. The boys were still up and excited about their rescue. Needless to say we got rid of our car soon after as it never fully recovered.

My nervous breakdown happened around here so the advice below is following on from this.

You may have a false impression of the past which can make you feel guilty. I was looking through my photos yesterday and even though as described in my last book, I felt like I had neglected my children somewhat (whilst I was training to teach and during my four years as a teacher), all I could see were happy times and faces. I realised that mainly I had neglected myself over this time and then felt less guilty.

I found photos were also good for seeing how far you have come since having mental health problems. I look at photos and remember how anxious I had felt in that time and then compare it to how I feel now and that helps me, because I can tell I am getting better. It might also help to talk to people as you may feel you came across differently to how you actually did. For example you may feel you came across as stressed out or silly in a situation and people may not have seen that at all.

Making special memories is so important. After all, these can be passed on, shared and remembered when you are separated from friends and loved ones. It can be simple memories like the time we stopped a magpie attacking another bird. We got the bird into a box. When we lifted it up we were pondering what to do with it when it squawked and flew out of the box. We talked about it after and although we didn't have a photo, I remember my son's delighted face when the bird flew up past him. This one shows you don't have to spend lots of money to have special memories.

Don't be too precious about your belongings when you first get them. This seems to be worse if you have OCD or anxiety. Mine stems from the worry of the cost to replace things and the hassle. I remember when we got our table for the garden. It was pristine. We had put some oil on it to protect it. But the oil had gone a bit blotchy so I had sanded it down again with Mum and Dad's help. But in the end with time the table had become weathered even with a cover on in the winter. It was teak and in a way it was fine for it to go grey with time. I guess again this was a control issue. I couldn't stop things aging or getting worn or even damaged. I had to appreciate that distressed furniture was in fashion again. If you haven't damaged anything on purpose then you hadn't done anything wrong.

Don't be in a rush to open something when it arrives but equally don't put things off. Anxiety can breed anxiety. For example you might be in a rush to do something and get it over with due to anxiety and then you might end up worrying because you damaged it. This happened when my son's guitar arrived. I was so keen to get it out and check it, I didn't realise there was metal inside the box. I then worried because I might have scratched the guitar. Or you might worry too much so that you avoid doing something and then worry about the effect this has.

Make the best out of things. A canal holiday we went on one Easter would have, to most people, seemed like a disaster. When we headed off we should have realised the river flow was strong when the man from the boathouse failed to turn the boat and it lay across the river, stuck at each end. My husband and I were at the bow and put the boat hook into the bank to help turn it. The boat started to move and my husband couldn't get the pole out quick enough and it snapped. Luckily we were not hurt. In the end a small boat had to come and help us turn. My sister took a picture of it and promptly put it on Facebook.

Finally we could head off down the canal and we negotiated a lock successfully. We were soon going under a bridge and I noticed how high the water was and those of us out on the boat had to duck dramatically to get through. I turned round to Dad and said, 'That was low'. We were just getting the hang of it but decided to stop at a meadow the boatman had recommended as it was dinner time. We moored up with the mooring pins and ropes. It was just before another lock and weirs.

When we woke in the morning Mum commented on the fast flow of the river and said we wouldn't be going anywhere today. It was true, someone from the boatyard had come to tell us not to move due to insurance and safety purposes. My dad tried his best to get him to let us move the next day but the man was firm. To be honest I could see how quickly the river was flowing and I imagined how the boat may end up going the wrong way and if one of us fell in it would be serious. So we decided to make the best of it.

Where we were on the River Wey meant we could get off and walk into Guildford. We visited the castle and museum, had lunch and visited the shops. On one of the later days when flooding was still high, my sons, nephew and I went for a muddy walk. All of a sudden two deer were right in front of us and then ran across to the right. It was amazing and we wouldn't have seen them on the boat. I was too slow with my camera but my son managed to find their tracks and we took a picture of these. In the end we had made the best of it all and safety was a key factor and it was good to foresee dangers but not to get obsessed by them. I had managed to keep away thoughts of the fast-flowing river and our mooring lines coming loose, for example. We had been extra careful around the banks of the canal.

Make sure you communicate with your partner, husband, wife. The other day a familiar topic of conversation had come up. I was arranging for my friend to come and see me whilst I was off sick. My husband had said they'd need to be quiet as he was on nights. This got me going – 'another way I have to run my life around your shifts', 'I have to do things with just me and the boys at weekends a lot'. At this point we had a few cross words that I don't really remember. To be honest I had become independent as I couldn't rely on my hubby being off work when we were. But he did say he wanted to do more with us but whenever he asked we didn't feel like it. I was surprised at this and said days out require planning and I'd get on to it right away. We had both made sacrifices for each other's jobs and I'm glad we sorted it out. We have done a lot more together since.

Get a second opinion if you still think something is wrong. In 2016 I had noticed my tremor in my left hand had got worse. I would be at a training session at work where you line up and make your own hot drink out of an urn. I noticed when I used a spoon I would shake uncontrollably and spill coffee or sugar. People had started to notice. So I booked a doctor's appointment.

When I got there I explained what was happening and that I was worried it might be Parkinson's as it runs in my family. I remember the doctor who later turned out to be a cardiologist asked me to put my left hand out. He then placed a piece of paper on my hand. From this he said it wasn't Parkinson's and that I didn't seem to have a resting tremor. I was prescribed propranolol, a beta blocker. So off I trotted to try the tablets. I found that they didn't really help my tremor and if anything gave me heart palpitations. I gave it over six months but returned to another doctor.

She, on my insistence, referred me to a neurologist. ECGs had been shown to the previous doctor. He had recommended as mentioned earlier coming off caffeine which reduced my palpitations significantly. When I met my neurologist I was immediately impressed. She was clearly passionate and knowledgeable about my possible condition. She got me to do various things with my arms and I could feel that my left side was slower than my right. My tremor was bad at this first meeting, probably because afterwards I had to attend a funeral of a friend. My neurologist booked me in for two brain scans and some blood tests.

MRIs always made me nervous, so I took the precaution of being prepared and strapped some absorbent felt with lavender oil drops on just below my nose. It was either that or getting prescribed Valium which would probably knock me out as much as Primidone (a tablet I had tried for my tremor) had a month or so before. I coped quite well and without the lavender in the end, although it was too much for me to operate the locker as I had put my glasses in there. Once the machine was running and clicking and beeping I was glad there was a mirror to see the operatives. I managed to keep my thoughts away from being buried alive and being in a submarine with no real escape.

The later DaT scan was critical to my diagnosis as the MRI scan had only picked up a sinus issue, but even this scan had made me anxious. The nurses and radiographers were great though. When you first see them they measure you and then give you iodine tablets, so that you don't absorb the radioactive tracer in your thyroid gland. I remember going for a coffee to let the tablets take effect and worrying that I may not have swallowed all of one of the tablets and it was still in the cup. You then go back for the injection, wait a while and then have your scan. For this you have to lie on a very narrow bench. Your head facing up and surrounded by a white arch-like structure that moves around to carry out the scan. It was all rather space age. You are told that you must keep your head absolutely still for what could be 45 minutes. I think it was 40 minutes in the end. There was a radio to listen to and I lay there worrying if I would sneeze or cough. I suddenly had the urge to look if my bag was safe where I thought I had put it. In the end I managed to keep my head still. It turned out that this was good as the abnormalities were not immediately obvious to the consultant until they looked at the data.

Keep looking for answers. In my last book I had explained how my increased dopamine levels due to stress had caused my psychosis. Now I had started to think what had come first for me, my Parkinson's or my nervous breakdown? Had one of these caused the other? It was a bit like the chicken or the egg question. So I looked into it on the web. I am now thinking that my likely high levels of dopamine in 2011 may have brought on Parkinson's earlier than my genetics was going to.

It turns out that dopamine itself can stress out nerve cells if it is in too higher amounts [4]. They had become 'stressed out' like humans do, the cells had a mitochondrial dysfunction and were suffering from oxidative stress [1]. My dopamine-making nerve cells were possibly dying off as a result, as shown in my DaT scan for Parkinson's. If you remember from school science, mitochondria are the cell structures where respiration occurs, producing energy for cells for different purposes. So if these are affected the cells could die.

This cartoon of a nerve cells shows that if we become overstressed our cells can become stressed too.

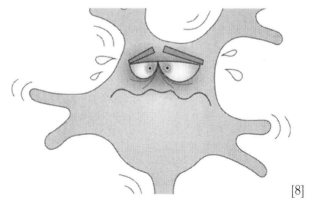

[8]

But for stress to have caused the Parkinson's it would need to affect only the nerve cells of the substantia nigra pars compacta (SNpc). Possibly this is because of an increased uptake of dopamine in that brain area, during high stress. Or it could be because these cells are more likely to produce the toxic form of dopamine [10]. It is all rather mind blowing as certain T cells that normally protect the body can kill nerve cells too, and cortisol, as mentioned in my earlier book, can have a part to play.

An argument for the Parkinson's coming first is that the mental health symptoms I experienced in my breakdown and beyond are listed in the symptoms of Parkinson's. These symptoms are anxiety, depression, psychosis and even apathy [7].

Anxiety for people with Parkinson's is believed to be caused by an imbalance of brain chemicals [13]. When looking into psychosis I was confused; as stated in my first book high levels of dopamine could cause psychosis and Parkinson's acts to reduce dopamine levels. The link between psychosis and Parkinson's was in fact due either to the medication for Parkinson's or dementia which I did not have in 2011 [12].

So Parkinson's did not explain my psychotic episode in 2011 (eight years before my diagnosis and medication). However, the anxiety from early Parkinson's could have helped send me over the edge in my breakdown. I had always wondered why I had been so vulnerable to stress.

The NHS site [9] lists stress, lack of sleep and Parkinson's as possible causes of psychosis. I'm still not entirely sure which came first but the main thing is I have a diagnosis (which I got at 44 years old – that's young according to my nice neurologist) and can now get help and treatment.

Friends had been concerned about the diagnosis for me but I knew if I had something it was better to know what it was so that I could tackle it head on and to get any benefits I was entitled to. Yes, I had been in tears about it all but that was just the initial shock. I feel that 'the genes may load the gun and the environment or another unknown factor may pull the trigger' [14] when it comes to getting Parkinson's. My twin sister does thankfully not show the signs of it yet, so I think the stress of teaching and not looking after myself may have been the environmental factor in my case. Either way stress is not healthy; studies are starting to show the link between stress and Parkinson's.

My new tablets for Parkinson's were helping with anxiety I remember one of my main concerns with getting new tablets was 'would I still be able to drink beer?' I asked this question when the consultant said that I should take Rasagiline. I had tried converting to non-alcoholic beer. But it just didn't taste right. I won't say here what my dad used to call weak beer. I would just listen to his advice. 'One good drink was better than lots of bad drinks'. The tablets work by inhibiting an enzyme that normally breaks down dopamine to make up for the lower amount of dopamine produced as a result of Parkinson's [11].

I was now also on the flu jab list as Parkinson's can make you more vulnerable, this explains some of my sickness over the past few years at least. I also got tired very quickly and that word fatigue keeps popping up on Parkinson's websites.

Look for role models. My auntie is 84 and also has Parkinson's. I look to her a lot to see how she is coping and she is doing really well. It gives me hope that I will be OK at that age too. She has only just recently given up driving and now zooms around on a mobility scooter. She does have difficulties but she takes them in her stride. Another older role model is Captain Sir Tom. He has shown what a contribution older people can have to society; with the words of BBC News 'He had wise words and modesty that the country needed in lockdown'. I think it is also important to try and be a role model yourself too and use your experiences to help others.

Listen to your consultant. A year ago I was suffering with a few health problems and not just my mental health. I was due to have a hysterectomy. Since when had I become afraid of general anaesthetic? I'd had at least four operations before with no problems. But I remember when I woke up from my one in 1999 one of the nurses said they had lost five that day.

I know I could have been imagining it or got the wrong end of the stick but it was now ingrained on my brain. I had got so worked up about the upcoming hysterectomy I had become ill. I was tired on the day but otherwise felt OK. One of the nurses had measured my temperature and it was high but it was hot in there. Anyway, nurse after nurse and doctor after doctor came to see me with forms to fill in. I started to panic a bit thinking of the general anaesthetic and the spinal and stomach injections they were going to do. The questions kept on coming and coming: 'Would it be OK if I had a blood transfusion?', 'Would it be OK to take a picture of the removed organs?' My heart rate was pretty high due to all of this. Luckily they did measure my temperature again before they took me down to theatre; it was 38.8°C even on a second thermometer. They noticed my shaky hands and I said I was having other tests for that but a nurse and I noticed I was clammy on my arms. For safety they cancelled the operation. To begin with I just wished they'd put me out and done it, but when they mentioned I could go to intensive care with a temperature like that if operated on I got the picture.

I got myself straight to the GP and she tested my urine for signs of infection. Even before we got home a prescription had been written. The infection turned out to be quite nasty and I was really glad the team had decided not to operate. I had seen my husband ill with an infection in hospital and that was enough for me.

I think part of the problem with my worry about the impending operation was it was my first operation since my nervous breakdown. In the end it took four prescriptions including two different antibiotics and lots of rest to beat my infection. One of the nurses asked me how my mental health was and I replied, 'Not very good' with a tearful voice. She said, 'Well you have got a lot on at the moment'. Which was true, I had been waiting for two brain scans to try to determine what was causing my shaky hand and other tests before my operation. We talked about my medication and I headed off to work before getting ill again after a week. At least three weeks on and the antibiotics had given me a good break from alcohol. Almost 60% of us have been using alcohol to cope with the stress of life [5]. I didn't want to be part of that anymore.

Don't forget to treat yourself. Otherwise what is the point? I looked forward to my oil order every month. Lavender was good for relaxing me and I enjoyed trying the other oils. I attempted to put out of my mind that with Parkinson's you sometimes lose your sense of smell. I would take out more time for me. It's great to be kind to other people but you have to be kind to yourself too.

Sleep, sleep, sleep. This is so important. You can't store up sleep to use at another time so don't get rundown. I think lockdown brought us more sleep and as a result we were relaxed and rested and clear, creative thinkers. I looked forward to my cat's little stays in the cattery as I wouldn't get woken up early to let her out and feed her. The other day I had a conversation with her. I told her it was not appropriate to bring in a wiggly worm at 6am and meow loudly letting us all know. When you have young children (or cats) go back to bed when you can. I have read that you can 'over' sleep. I don't really think that is possible in our busy world!

Accept support and help others. A senior manager at school approached me about women's health. She was very supportive and messaged me whilst I was in hospital. We were both going through similar things, the fear of the general anaesthetic and the spinal block for example. We continued to support each other looking at the funny side at times. Hot flushes often came up and a funny magnet I had bought from a local shop had compared them to power surges.

If you can, find work that you can also do from

home. I think you can be more creative at home. Why had I not discovered Zoom meetings before now? Initially I was a bit nervous about them. The circle would spin round after you joined the meeting and then bam you're in there. One meeting when I had clicked on the video icon on the left. I exclaimed 'My hair'. The cat had also disturbed work Zoom meetings and my husband asking when I wanted lunch. But it was all good as we were muted during any important bits. It was funny when people changed their backgrounds. One meeting someone had a Hawaiian shirt to match the palm trees in the background. Another one had various backgrounds which were changed, one with piles of toilet roll in. But seriously I think the world is going to lean more towards working from home for various reasons.

If you only have about 10 years left at work make sure it suits you. My dad was a good example of this. He had worked for Ford for as long as I could remember. He had his battles there and would come back from work to bash the hell out of something in the shed as stress relief. I had noticed for his last 10 years there he had enjoyed it more and had even been able to go on track days testing out various cars as part of his work. He was definitely happier. There is a balance; you need to make a living but you need to also enjoy living.

You might surprise yourself. I had started to appreciate my job more when redundancy had loomed its ugly head again for me. It seemed just as I had settled into work I may have to look for other work. In my second meeting the HR lady from the trust was there again. At the start she talked about the redundancy still going ahead and I had said that I now realised my role was going. I then said, 'If there is a school that needs support staff it is this one'. She said the trust would consider me for similar roles that would come up in the partner schools. I said, 'That's good but actually I quite like working here'. As I said this I thought of how hard I had found it working there. But things were getting better and I understood the students' needs better than when I started. The staff were amazing to work with and it would be hard to replace that. After this meeting there was hope that I could stay on in a different role. More about this later.

Looking back I ask myself why did I allow myself to get stressed out by people or work? This kind of links into the advice below. I'd been through quite a lot at each of my workplaces but I carried on and by the large part things had improved. There was a balance between not being a pushover and keeping your head down. All the time you had to be strong. Once you have found something that suits you stick with it.

Other people's opinions or comments are just that. I remember one of my friend's exes being rather rude at our wedding – commenting about how late the buffet for evening guests was. I found out later at my 27th birthday at a pub lock-in that he was generally rude anyway. This time I had successfully ignored it and we had a great time dancing on the tables! When I had decided to change jobs, a work colleague said, 'What could you teach?' implying with their tone that I wasn't very knowledgeable. Needless to say I declined their later friend request on social media. Yes there is still some bitterness there and writing this paragraph is like therapy. If you've done nothing wrong it is generally their problem and you shouldn't let it impact on your happiness. I was learning to not blow things out of proportion but this can be hard and remember not to dwell on these moments.

This one links to the one above. **It's what the people close to you think of you that really matters.** Now I don't mean that you can ignore what other people might think and run naked down your street. I mean that you shouldn't over-worry about what people think about you. If the people close to you (both friends and family) think the world of you that's what really matters. Don't be too hard on yourself.

If you need help ask for it. I was reminded of this when my youngest shaved without shaving foam as he didn't realise he needed it. He ended up cutting himself. If no one is there to help there is always YouTube or Google!

Hold onto hope. Entering competitions was always a good one for this. I had recently entered a photo competition and even though there was no prize as far as I could see, it would be great to get in the top 100. This would give recognition. Currently I had renewed hope for the school. A much needed new building was nearing completion and this would be a real boost. I always had the hope that my books would eventually sell and get noticed and I had new hope of getting a 'bolthole' of some kind.

Your limits don't have to be the same as other people's. It is good sometimes to be encouraged to do things, but don't feel pressured to. If you want a lazy morning at the weekend then have one. With most families working all the time it is important to get some reset time. Pressure can come from social media. You can end up looking at all the activities that your friends are doing and feel like you should be doing more at the weekends or in the evening. You do what is best for you and your family.

Other ways to avoid the pitfalls of social media. Social media is part of everyday life now and for all its pitfalls it is the only way I keep in touch with some people, either due to geographical reasons or other reasons. It is the only way I have found out about three deaths, for example. On a happier side it can be useful for good news and sparking up conversations when you do finally meet people in the flesh.

It has caused me a bit of anxiety in the past when people have taken my posts the wrong way. This was for only two out of thousands of posts, thankfully. But you do have to be sensible with your posts. It is probably best to avoid any politics on there. Another thing to avoid are emojis when the conversation is serious or requires empathy as you can accidently touch an inappropriate emoji and it will send automatically before you can do anything about it! Also remember potential employers can see your profiles and often search for people's names before hiring.

Heated exchanges should be avoided while driving. Those who know me realise I don't get angry very easily but

I have on a couple of occasions got angry in the car due to a conversation which has annoyed me. Once with my sister I had slammed on the brakes (looking in the mirror first) to prove a point. I had wanted to do this the other day after a conversation about my mental health and how it all started but I managed to hold it together. Leave conversations that could cause anger until you are out of the car and pick up the signs when you have annoyed someone. In fact, driving should always be a relaxed affair. Maybe I should use my car oil diffuser more, it fits into the fan vent to release relaxing aromas.

Pick a partner/wife/husband that loves the jobs you hate. This sounds like a Mr Muscle advert but it really makes sense. If you both like cooking but hate cleaning, who is going to do the years of cleaning or ironing? It makes teamwork much easier if you have your own little niches. I had found it strange when a friend and his family had visited years back and said 'Come on, team' when it was time for them to go. But I get it now. In our case my husband does the cooking. This is for the best as I have served up cardboard before under an en croute and although I can cook to an extent I turn into Keith Floyd and need a glass of wine next to me if it is for an extended amount of time.

Writing these points down has definitely been good therapy in itself.

This is only advice and you know what is best for you, everyone will have different experiences and it is good to talk. My grandmother used to have sayings which were useful; 'A change is as good as a rest', 'A little of what you fancy does you good' and 'Count your blessings' for example. These relate to what I have found about mental health. I would find myself saying them now and again; 'It never rains but it pours' and 'You live and learn'. Many things come with a risk, even simple things. I am in pain now as I had shut my car door hard into my knee. I'm not sure how but it had been hard enough for me to hear a crack and feel quite a lot of pain. Part of me felt that if I could do that much damage by doing something like that, what would it have been like if I fell off a scooter with flip-flops on, for example. The other part of me thought, well I might as well get out there and have some fun again. I had my motorbike licence but that was before my anxiety really hit.

The next part of the book looks at how I am taking back some control over anxiety by writing and describes how I have found the whole self-publishing journey.

Part 3
The Writing Journey

So how had my writing journey begun?

I still remember a story I wrote at primary school about waking up and not being able to see until my eyes had been washed. It must have been quite a short story but I remember trying to put my emotions into the story. The fear and worry that I may not see again. The arduous journey to the bathroom and then, trying to find the sink. I had always been a worrier. I'm not sure if I remember the story because the teacher thought it was good or because it made me think quite a lot to write it. I must have been about six or seven.

Success did come when I designed a poster for a competition judged by Spike Milligan. I got fifth prize. The poster was to celebrate the end of the war. I remember drawing people around a piano singing. My short poem was top-left it read 'Royal Britannia Marmalade and Jam, Hitler is dead, now we can all have some ham'. I had come up with this caption myself, short but catchy. I went into the school hall and all the entrants' posters were on display for our school and mine had a little note on it. I didn't get to keep the poster but I got the *Ghostbusters* soundtrack on a couple of cassettes. I also kept a diary for a short while when I was about 11 but I didn't write anything too personal in it in case my sister or Mum read it.

My first book had gone to a publisher with offices in London and New York. I had had emails from them saying the quality of the writing was good and could I add to it. So I added Part 2. They then said they needed more so I added Part 3. All the time I was becoming hopeful that they would take the book on. Eventually they said they would accept the book but I would need to contribute £2700 of my own money. They had reduced the cost a little and stated 'We sincerely hope you'll consider our offer so we can help get your fascinating memoir into the public eye where it deserves to be'. I had decided it was too much money to risk and luckily my sister had a contact of an author who helped new authors and writers to self-publish. It became increasingly obvious to me that successful books were more possible for celebrities and people with lots of money to spare. I felt determined to do my best to market my books; after all, how many celebrities had spent two weeks in a mental health ward and had struggled with everyday challenges in poorly funded schools? I was still thankful for the feedback from the publishers which after all had motivated me to keep going with my writing.

It was a bit daunting when I first thought about marketing my book. I think I had this false belief that a good book would just sell itself. Well I called it a book, my husband jokingly called it a pamphlet as it was only 90 pages long. It is true that you have to believe in your product, but every day, really, you should be thinking about getting your book out there. Even on a holiday to France thoughts came up.

We had arrived at our lovely gite after a mega journey with a delay at the Folkestone tunnel. My son noticed there were books to read under the TV. I said, 'I could have brought my book along and left it here so people read it'. He picked up one of the books and said, 'This author did the same'. It was a Ruth Rendell book and I couldn't help laughing. 'She is a very well-known author. I don't think she would have left it here,' I said. I also found a magazine and noted contact details in case they wanted to do a story on my book. I don't seem to have much luck with magazines which is strange as my story had been quite dramatic. In the Ruth Rendell book I had found one error (earth the planet should have had a capital E in my opinion). This also reassured me as I had found one in my first book, but this had been in a student's quotation marks so it wasn't too bad.

I had been invited to a Wellbeing Symposium after approaching Wellbeing People about my book. I took my mum along for moral support. I felt it was a bit jinxed at first as the road we were going to use was closed as a body had been found on it the evening before. Luckily Mum knew this so we went a different way and set off a bit earlier.

The traffic was heavy and when we finally approached the hotel sirens were going off everywhere. It was enough for anyone with anxiety. Still, we managed to park and set up a stall in the entrance area. I had a few books, pens, business cards and objects which represented my crisis point, such as the colouring I had done in hospital, some shoes and a film board. It was good to talk to those running it and to the people who had come along to the event. I really enjoyed the talks and wondered if I would ever pluck up the courage for public speaking. One particular talk was on happiness at work and I got a few pointers from that. A highlight of the day was when I was given a name badge with 'Samantha Glynn Author' on. I was chuffed to say the least. I also got positive feedback about the book from someone at Wellbeing People which was great.

At the moment I am feeling quite positive about getting people to notice my books and I've had the following additional achievements.

1) The Mental Health Book Club have read my book and given positive feedback and are looking forward to reviewing it. I will need to do a podcast interview for that. I'm feeling excited and anxious about that but they do give you some heads up on the questions. Unfortunately nothing has materialised from this yet but they still follow me on Twitter.

2) I contacted the Recovery and Wellbeing College and they were very interested in my experience and came round to collect a copy of the book and some business cards that I had. It was good talking to the NHS lead. I found that my face started to twitch with what must have been nerves but I held it together. It would be great if I could one day become

a peer trainer. She sent me a document that was written by psychologists on the topic of psychosis. It took me a while to read the 100-page document but I found that what I had written in my book agreed with what they had written. The personal experiences of survivors of mental health were also honest like mine and I was horrified to find that due to many ward closures some spend time in a police cell; this must be very scary.

3) My book had eventually made it into Margate Library. It had taken a visit and a few reminder emails to get it into the wellbeing section. At times it seemed there was little help out there to get noticed as another library had told me they couldn't help market my book but that they would gladly take one of my marketing pens!

4) A small local charity (The Solve Charity for Mental Health) had emailed me back and I could see myself doing a presentation on my experiences for them. After all, I was used to standing up in front of people for work.

So having successes did mean I would have to take it easy a bit. I would be conscious of lying in bed worrying about being hauled into the office at work for writing about how bad it had been. Someone had got my book out of their bag in the early days in the staffroom and I had thought 'oh no' (or words to that effect, if you know what I mean) but luckily they had quickly put it back. Management would find out soon as people from work were finally getting time to read it and were passing on how much they liked it. Or I would find myself wondering what a new contact was thinking about my book. I had to stop this as sleep was essential for me. So I told my husband I was going to have a break from marketing for a while. I still kept on with my Facebook and Twitter accounts; although my total number of followers wasn't high I didn't want to disappoint. I found my Voice for Anxiety page helped me too as it encouraged me to find more ways to help beat anxiety. It always pleased me when more people liked my Voice for Anxiety page. I never seemed to run out of things to put on it.

Of course it would be good to break into the American market. I've had limited success there. Well that is to say I have had a couple of sales! I have had contact with Psychcentral and they have got a link for my anxiety page as a support group. Also, I sent my book to Mental Health America but in the end they couldn't help. It would be good if I could go to America and do a book launch similar to what Ruby Wax describes in her book *Frazzled*. But the thought of going to America on my own with anxiety does not fill me with confidence.

Once, a few years back, we were sat down having dinner and one of my boys started talking about his bedtime reading. 'Dad says I should read proper books when I'm in bed not annuals... I could read Mum's book'. Another family member nearly choked on her pasta. I didn't see this as annoying more like amusing as I knew my book wasn't like a full-length novel that so many people see as a proper book.

During a break from work I had time to look into marketing my book more. I had contacted Amazon and although I had done some things right, there was still more to do to market my book effectively:

1) I had tried the book promotions available such as free ebooks for a limited time or reducing the cost of my book for a limited time. But only the free ebooks had limited success. This was probably because my book wasn't coming up in searches despite being linked to keywords when it was set up. These keywords included stress and anxiety for example. The ad campaigns help books to appear in searches but a budget would need to be set as costs could spiral.

2) I was originally wary of Amazon ads. I felt nervous when I set it up online. My first campaign had only shown once with no clicks. I was going to keep doing small budgets until I was getting clicks and sales – after all, you only paid when someone clicked on the ad. One of my friends had phoned up and others had messaged me saying well done after reading my first book and asking why I was still in

education. He had known me all my life and said that I had always seemed calm.

To me anxiety is deep-rooted and can be hidden taking large amounts of energy. My relatives in America had even written in a Christmas card that my book had helped them. Someone had messaged me and it made me quite emotional. She had written, 'I've been taking my time reading your book but wanted to thank you. I've had an awful 18 months and it really helped to put things into perspective'. I was hoping more people could find my book. At the moment the search in Amazon seemed to only come up with my book if they knew my name or some of the title.

Keywords had been set up as mentioned but it seemed like advertising campaigns were needed for these to be more successful. I have decided to put the word anxiety in my title for this book in the hope that it will appear in the search for this word on the Amazon site without the need for ad campaigns. Other books came up when the word anxiety was searched for and it would be great to see mine pop up on the screen. This book was going to be called *Moving forward and writing out my Bread Crumb List* so maybe this simple change of adding the word anxiety will help. An author's name is good to search for but as I am not a celebrity I do not have a profile that reaches lots of people.

At least now after some adjustment on the publishing site I could see all my paper book sales which were for a short time showing nothing. I was also thankful that I hadn't figured out how to order author copies until now. It made my sales graph look a bit more acceptable when I went into the Amazon Kindle Direct Publishing site. There was clearly some work still to be done. After two automatic campaigns with no sales, or cost luckily, I decided to be brave enough to attempt the manual option for advertising with Amazon. Once selected I realised I should have been brave enough to do this before although I wasn't clear on the options for the keywords, such as broad. I could easily add anxiety, stress, psychosis, mental health books, nervous breakdown and stress of teaching. This campaign again had no clicks so I took a plunge and decided to write one for Amazon.com.

One night I got a click. I was so excited when I got this! It may not have meant a sale (I will check this at the end of the 10 days) but at least someone had seen it. It had cost just over $2 as I had set the bid above the ones that had come up automatically as that cost wasn't working. I had adjusted the keywords to have 'book' at the end but kept them broad. Next time I would use the phrase 'Stressed teacher' too. My husband had joked with me about the cost of one click and we had all had a laugh. But I was happy this one person may read my book, may like it, may write a review and may recommend it to others and it may help them.

The click had given me new hope as I was running out of ideas for marketing my book. I might have to contact my friend called the Marketing Bird. I had continued to use Facebook and Twitter to try to promote my book and I had recently figured out how to put a post with hashtags on Instagram. I didn't like the way that on Instagram people could start following you without giving you any information about them. A man with a photo that I presume was his had said 'Beautiful' on one of my posts and later 'How are you?' I know he may have been genuinely a nice guy with no romantic intentions but being married and slightly paranoid I didn't answer. With Twitter there was normally a description about the person and their interest in Anxiety/Mental Health. I also felt safer on Facebook as friends could be checked before they could see your posts.

It had occurred to me that I may have to become more 'aggressive' in my marketing. It was competitive out there and privileged in many ways. So whenever I could I would find a possible contact to email about my book. I would go through some of the successes mentioned above as well as describe the book. It is important to proofread your emails. Once I noticed I had written that I had a stool at the Wellbeing Symposium, rather than I had a stall! Luckily I hadn't sent the email at this point.

I recently started an Anxiety and Depression course with Future Learn which has helped me with ideas for this book. The course was very useful and showed me that how people saw things involved not only the eyes but the brain. Imagine a crowded beach scene... there have been quite a lot of those in the news lately. Imagine the people on the beach and those in the sea. How many good things popped up in your mind? How many negative things? The table below shows some things that could come to mind.

Positives	Negatives
'That looks like fun'	'There are too many people'
'Bet the water is lovely'	'I might drown'
'We could play ball games in the water'	'The water will be freezing'
'It is great to be outside'	'Someone will get lost in the crowd'
'I could snorkel'	'I'll get sunburnt'

Interestingly I look at the table now and I can see how some of the negatives have come from my past experiences. For instance I had got sunburnt on my back snorkelling on my honeymoon. Most people had been lost briefly in their lives and I had nearly drowned as described in my first book. I do tend to look at activities as a mini safety officer. I can still do this and put precautions in place and then just enjoy things. We are due to go to Corfu soon. Who knows if they have those rubber biscuit things which are large rubber rings behind a speedboat I may have a go, like I did when I was on a holiday with my sister when I was 18. Time to climb out of my bubble; avoidance only provides temporary relief.

I definitely would think about the threatening side which partly explains my anxiety. It is good to be wary of the dangers but these thoughts need to be controlled. Sometimes you have to reason with yourself. Future Learn asked why I was doing the course. I selected 'other' as this allowed me to put that I had a Facebook page and I was looking at the suitability of the course for myself and my followers. They didn't need to know that at this time of writing I had around 40 followers not thousands. I suddenly realised that this may be the way to approach marketing in the future. I didn't like being pushy but simply having a book that I know helped people won't get it out there. Even writing these things down has made me realise who I needed to chase up. It was another good reason to hoard all emails, as I do.

There was always hope that my first book would become a cult book or a short film. I still felt psychosis was misunderstood and needed more realistic coverage. So I had searched for real-life experience books on psychosis and found one called *Brain on Fire*. It had, in fact, been made into a film, so I would need to try and see that at some point. I was interested to know how the author had got her message out there. She had appeared on *This Morning*. I couldn't quite picture myself doing that, it was outside my comfort zone. Her psychosis had been caused by an infection and she had recovered well. I found that she worked for the *New York Times* so I put some of her success down to this and didn't feel too bad about my book. Joining a psychosis forum on Facebook I had started to learn that causes can vary so much but sleep seemed to be one of the common factors. I know I hadn't been taking care of my bodily needs when mine started. How much sleep and food you had come up on the UCL Covid-19 survey I was doing which clearly looked at mental health. My sleep had been OK although I was finding it harder to get to sleep during lockdown and sleeping in until about 9.

During the pandemic my sister pointed me towards a poetry competition. It was to write about nature as experienced by you. It took about a day to write and think about. It was based around my dream to get a small area of a woods. Lockdown had provided further evidence for me that it was time to get a 'bolthole' somewhere to get away from crowds in this crazy world. I could imagine our family and friends camping there and sitting around a camp fire. I had even thought of getting a composting toilet and tool shed if this was allowed. I had a few niggling worries such as footpaths running near the woods, fly tipping, invasions, accidents or even fire. But then I thought of the benefits such as those for mental health and managing the woods would bring valuable experience for my sons. They could learn to coppice and I could imagine my youngest using myForest from the Royal Forestry Society to map it all out and catalogue it. My son and I had recently watched *The Dead Don't Die* as we had started watching weekly horror films. Unlike the film *Hush* it had shown that woods were a safe place to be. Anyway, here is the poem:

Nature in the Air

It was like a big realisation,
Covid-19 had showed me to look after nature,
Being out of the car and the rat race gave me new sensation,
I began my journey by foot to my woods for the future,

I could hear the tree branches as they danced in the air,
Once in the woods I was away from the bustle,
Birds darted by me and all around and didn't care,
The leaves on the ground and my feet made a rustle,

I was happy here with nature around,
I took time to appreciate my vicinity and in that spot I could have stayed,
A squirrel looked at me and pranced on the ground,
The colours were bright even in this shade,

As I moved further into the woods the road noise started to fade,
The litter on the floor was natural and clean,
To my right I saw a ring that the mushrooms had made,
Looking back I could no longer see where I had been,

Stepping forward a few steps I stopped all of a sudden,
I was in awe as before me stood two deer, they turned their heads then started to shift,
They were beautiful creatures and my eyes followed them until they were hidden,
I felt a wave of gratitude moments like this were a gift,

Blue bells* were all around I could smell their sweet scent,
I decided no rush to leave,
Breathe, Breathe, Breathe.

To me this was it everyone deserved their piece of nature…

Covid-19 had turned out to be a horrendous disease and in my heart I had always known it would be worse than flu. People seemed to get seriously ill very quickly and it wasn't always the older and weaker. Viral load seemed to be a big factor and I'm sure there will be other books written about the lack of PPE and the mistakes made.

Our concerned Headteacher had sent me home early with other vulnerable members of staff. I remember my anxiety peaked when the UK death toll hit 100 and my sons were still at school. I also remember whilst clapping for the NHS a police car drove by slowly and they were wearing masks. Later we would wear masks and think nothing of it. I had become more aware of sirens and would find these a reminder of the virus even though it may not have been linked to each siren I heard.

The disease had shown that whilst this horror was unleashed, the world was healing with humans out of the way for a while. I'd heard that CO_2 levels had dropped and air quality has improved. Lions were napping on roads free from traffic in Africa, dolphins had returned to Venice and now Hong Kong, goats had taken over towns in Wales and mice had been spotted dancing on an Underground platform! I had particularly liked the pictures and videos of Arnold Schwarzenegger in lockdown with his donkeys in his house having breakfast.

I was pretty pleased with my poem and feedback from friends and family (as ever) was good. I sent it off in PDF format with my brief history of writing poems. That night like so many in lockdown I had trouble getting to sleep. *I suddenly thought blue bells should be all one word! I checked in the morning and it was. Why had I not noticed this? Well it wouldn't be picked up by the spell-checker and it sounded right. Thinking about it further it was a happy mistake the bells related to my time teaching in school and stress moving from lesson to lesson. I started to think I had no chance of winning. I think you should never really analyse your own poems too much! The competition also said that it would be for a shadow puppet animation of no less than three minutes. I decided to record it reading aloud. It came to one minute 54 seconds. Again I started to doubt my chances and even thought of two more verses to add and send in.

After gift I could insert the following:

…Walking again I came to a clearing,
Busy and preoccupied butterflies and bees were carrying out their important roles,
From flower to flower they flew sometimes disappearing,
Spinning free with my arms out stretched I nearly fell in some hidden holes,

Giggling to myself thinking of the animals that slept beneath,
What they must think of human intrusions,
I imagined their thick furry coats as they peered out in disbelief,
I quickly jumped up over the years I'd lost my delusions,

Up ahead between the trees came a shallow stream,
In and out of the ragged roots it bent,

Imminent blue bells…

I read the call out brief for the poem again and it said a short poem of no longer than two pages. So I decided not to send the extra material in. If they liked it they liked it and I would just have to wait. The extra work had taken ages and didn't seem to flow as well as the original poem and if anything it had changed the mood. Still, if they did ask for a longer version it was ready.

When writing poems I found it was probably best to go with your gut instinct and what initially comes in the first day. It is weird when creativity hits. For this poem it was when I was sat waiting for a call from my line manager about my performance management meeting. Luckily I had a notebook to hand.

Notebooks were also essential for writing larger texts such as a book of 26,000 words. I would often write something and then come back to it after thinking of more to write whilst in various places, shower, etc. Only occasionally have I written something that I couldn't fathom out later. There is definitely something such as writer's block.

I tried to get on the computer as soon as I felt in the mood to write. Sometimes the computer wasn't free but I would get on it again when I could. Short spurts of writing would mean that I would need to sit down and tweak the document near the end so that it flowed in a particular order, this had been one of the negative feedbacks in a rare review from a stranger on my first book. I would print my first complete draft out and check that the order was better and the flow was easy to follow, this was quite difficult to do on a computer screen. To be fair there was a lot going on in my first book.

There was satisfaction that came with writing. I would knock out a few paragraphs and look bottom left to see my word count increasing. I don't think I will ever write a very long book though. I was enjoying seeing this book come together and comments from friends such as 'can't wait to read it' spurred me on to get it published in a few months. After all, I had called it a series of books. Two books count, right? I looked forward to seeing the cover on my computer screen and receiving the first physical copy are exciting times for any writer.

I received an email for the poetry call out whilst I was online. Its title was 'update'. It took a while to open and part of me didn't want to read it. There had been nearly 200 entries and they explained the selection process which sounded fair and robust. Unfortunately mine hadn't made the short list or even the long list. It was a blow but I realised it was quite a personal poem and could have had more shadow screen potential. My words were a lot about feelings which would not be very visual. Part of me regretted not sending in the extra part. But as my sister says you can overwork a painting and it was good as it was. My son had said it was good but could have been more 'adult'. He didn't mean more X-rated but have more complex vocabulary!

I had enjoyed writing my poem and my friend had said that was the main thing. I have enjoyed writing these two books, or pamphlets as my husband calls them, and they have helped me gain some closure. It was funny when we were sent the winning poem on YouTube. It was professionally done but it did make me laugh. The finished work had included swear words and sexual indication which I had not expected to be allowed. My friends found this funny. Again I had got some closure as I had realised my work wasn't silly in its content it just needed to be more 'arty'. My son had been right in his statement! There had even been an image of a woman's breast. My poem, it appeared, had needed to be more 'risqué'.

With all this I had decided that poems were a good way to get messages about feelings out there. My school had worked hard on a virtual choir clip for students during lockdown. Something came to me that summed up how I felt about the situation. I came up with this simple sentence knowing that taking part in the singing was not a good idea – I had become increasingly tone deaf, my cat could sing better!

'Things have changed that is true, but we are still here for you!'

… It was true – teachers and staff were all doing a great job.

I had become increasingly proud of working at my school and I hoped to continue there in some capacity and lockdown had given me time to think about what I would do next. Whilst I had no desire to return to my previous hectic world, and the hectic world in general, I would take control and take one step at a time.

Lack of time had become a source of anxiety and I had

posted this on my Voice for Anxiety page.

There's that old saying 'time and tide waits for no man'. But to ease anxiety people needed time to breathe. I found I could think more clearly and creatively when I had more time and wasn't rushing around like a mad thing. Well it turned out I would have more time for a while.

My redundancy notice came through the post at the end of the first lockdown. It was nothing personal; the budget wasn't there for me to get a different role in the school, I found out. It was a hard time to be made redundant but I was confident I could get a part-time job and maybe continue writing as well. I updated my LinkedIn profile to 'looking for a job' and noticed that many of my contacts had posh job titles, 'Global Manager' for example. I thought about it for a while and simply put 'Tutor and Author' on mine with a wry smile. Well why not? At last I was able to do something that suited me and you should try not to compare yourselves with others although that is what I had done.

Shortly after my redundancy notice I had a bizarre dream. My dreams had always been vivid.

We were living in a different house and we were trying to secure the windows with string. There were people dressed up outside and ghouls going in a pub/restaurant next door. There was a snake in the garden that needed help shedding its skin, it was a rattlesnake and we avoided its head but it coiled up nicely in the end. Then we were looking out of our window and our son's phone went off. A tidal wave started and luckily our house floated. We could see a weird island. It all seemed to be controlled by phones.

It was time to look at Dream Bible again online. I produced the following table:

What I saw/did in the dream	Dream Bible meaning	Relating to how I feel	What I could do about it all
Window	'To dream of a window represents a perspective or insight on current events'.	I was quite emotional about redundancy and felt a loss of identity.	Find a new identity job wise. I still had an identity for family, friends, work experience/knowledge and hobbies.
Trying to secure windows	'To dream of a broken window represents lost opportunities or never getting to think about the future in a particular way ever again. Not feeling good about the future at all or feeling that an opportunity has been wasted'.	This was definitely how I felt about redundancy at this time. I didn't like change especially after my breakdown. The lost opportunity of working with some great colleagues in the Special Educational Needs department.	The future is not certain for anyone, not just me, and I had to remember that. I am a proactive person and things would be fine.
People in costumes and ghouls	'A ghoul in a dream may represent a petty unforgiving adversary who gets power from making sure you don't get to like yourself'.	I saw two flying in my dream. I can't think of anyone in particular, maybe one was my negative self that can haunt me by creating some negative thoughts.	Remember to like yourself and keep up those positive thoughts.

What I saw/did in the dream	Dream Bible meaning	Relating to how I feel	What I could do about it all
Rattlesnake	'To dream of a poisonous snake represents feelings about corruption or contamination. Snakes in dreams also tend to reflect a person's fear of total failure or serious losses'.	I did have a fear of the unknown that redundancy would bring.	I feel rested after lockdown and ready to take on the world again. I did feel I may lose focus, but I knew I had the focus of helping my sons with their important school years and finishing this book.
A light brown snake	'A positive opportunity to improve yourself that scares you'. 'To dream of fearing being bitten by a snake represents your fear of losing something important or a fear of total failure. You may fear losing power, control, safety, or your integrity'.	I did at this stage feel positive about online tutoring but would this last?	I had to remember that although I'd lost the safety net of my regular job. I still had lots to offer. I would take control and even be able to work part-time which is what I'd wanted for a long time. Fatigue did seem to hit me quite a lot from Parkinson's.
Snake shedding its skin	'Feelings of corruption that are not important or serious anymore'.	May link to past paranoia. Or feeling 'why me?' for redundancy.	The Headteacher had explained it was nothing personal and that was good enough for me. I'd handled it all rather well considering the problems with contracts in my last book.

What I saw/did in the dream	Dream Bible meaning	Relating to how I feel	What I could do about it all
Snake coiling up	This wasn't specifically on the Dream Bible site. I remember the snake being under control in the end. Ourselves as a family had controlled it.	I did feel like things were in control at home. Lockdown had given us the chance to regroup.	Yes we would have less money. But we could 'batten down the hatches'.
A tidal wave	'To dream of a tidal wave represents problematic life situations or uncertainty that threatens to overwhelm you emotionally'.	Sums it up really.	I will keep my emotions in check. The courses I had been doing will help with this and I had my oils which helped to ground me.
Weird brightly coloured island	'An island may point to situations where you feel independent, self-directed, and autonomous'.	I didn't feel very independent workwise yet but I was becoming more so.	My friends and family were confident I would do alright and that was a big help.

Looking at the Dream Bible site I wasn't the only one that was having strange dreams. What some people see through windows! The fact that my dream seemed to be all controlled by phones could be related to the 5G theory for Covid. Doing a table like the one above may help people even if they do not think dreams are related to feelings. It helped me a lot. Obviously don't get obsessed with it for every dream, just significant ones if you feel it helps. People may say 'you can read too much into dreams' but for me there was too much coincidence. Look out for bias. If I had watched *Snakes on a Plane* the night before the dream the connections would have been more dubious. There have been scientific studies using MRI technology for example on the link between dreams and emotions. 'Dreams are generated in, or transmitted through this particular area of the brain, which is associated with visual processing, emotion and visual memories'. [16]

Dreams actually help mental state and lack of REM sleep can have health consequences.

My course on Future Learn had told me in a nutshell why writing had been so good for my mental health.

It covered:

1) Behavioural activation
2) Psycho education

Behavioural activation means that people should make an effort to do what they enjoy when they are feeling low or anxious. The achievements that this brings will help break a vicious cycle. I enjoyed writing. I had also researched (i.e., carried out Psycho education) into the reasons for my mental illness for both of my books and this had helped me and others.

Everyone enjoys different things so they should concentrate on what they enjoy and what gives them a sense of achievement. I had liked the look of the zip-wire over the Welsh hills but I realise this may be a step too far and I might not enjoy it once I had launched. The course with Future Learn also explained that graded exposure can help people with phobias or anxiety. My initial nervousness with Zoom, which I think was quite common, is a good illustration of how you can take tiny steps to help. See the flow diagram below which shows my graded exposure. Luckily I wasn't presented with the highest difficulty first. It followed an order.

Least difficult in hierarchy

Introduced to Zoom by
group of 6 school friends

Zoom host with one friend. There were
a few audio problems but it was OK in
the end

Zoom with colleagues when I
don't have to speak

Small Zoom with colleagues where I
do have to speak or share screen

Zoom with large team of colleagues
(73) and have to speak! I must admit I
did have a beer after this

Most difficult in hierarchy

I now consider myself a bit of a Zoom Queen after getting through my first job interview on Zoom successfully and getting a place on the Academic Mentoring Scheme. I had avoided the 'I'm going to make a complete fool of myself' voice in my head.

I still get a bit anxious but I can do it! Having this book to write helped me identify the things that I have learned and that have helped me. I wasn't totally over anxiety as bouts of it could come and go but I understood it more now. Another sign of progress was seeing one of my 'baddies' from my first book. We had stopped to talk to each other about what we were doing now and I had no paranoid thoughts, it had taken a while but my conspiracy theory had been left behind. My future was looking good despite factors which were quite frankly out of my control.

Epilogue

The whole world had become like a film. Dad had told me on Skype it was like a sci-fi and that I had always liked sci-fi. I remember in March 2020 as the Corona virus hit I was feeling quite vulnerable walking down the crowded school corridors. Schools were where these sort of things spread very easily. It wasn't until it was announced that some staff had been told not to come in and stay off for 12 weeks that I realised how serious this was. My Headteacher had decided to take early action and for this I am very grateful. I had become rundown and when I was asked to go home too due to my Parkinson's I was relieved and resting up in the conservatory. Within two months I was feeling better. I worked from home over lockdown which had its own challenges but I learned a lot from it. Lockdown had eased my general anxiety. What would it be like when lockdown lifted?

One week after being sent home from school I decided to start completing a weekly survey for UCL on the effects of lockdown on mental health. It was one way of making myself useful. There were quite a few questions. Many directed at how I felt, for example did I feel hopeless or down? Other questions related to worries such as finances and getting seriously ill. Then you would let them know what activities you had been doing. Things like exercising, gardening and crafts were activities they seemed to expect to help with it all. One week I could tell my responses were more negative. That is because I had been worrying about finances. But in general my mental health had been good.

This is from my Voice for Anxiety page:

'I'm feeling calm. It has occurred to me that before all this my biggest worries were:

a) What if something happens to my family when they are out and about? (This is no longer a big worry as even my husband is working from home at the moment.)

b) Work used to worry me quite a bit (for example would I have to cover a full class of year 9? I am off work for 12 weeks).

c) Car journeys and parking (not happening at the moment).

d) Not spending enough time with my immediate family (not a problem now).

e) Not getting enough exercise (I have time for this now and we had a shed gym that had been finished at the start of lockdown).

I am not too worried about catching the virus at the moment as we are taking precautions and I may have already had it (at the start of February), but how will this all change when the lockdown ends?

Comments on this indicated that other people were feeling the same way too. I had also shared my experience of being locked in to Sapphire Ward in my first book *The Sapphire Conspiracy and beyond it all*. I could now see why the staff had allocated time in the small courtyard for us. We had also had activities organised for us such as quizzes, crafts, cooking and badminton.

During lockdown I had taken to baking. One of my successes was a lemon meringue cake which looked like Boris Jonson but tasted good. I could totally see why Nadiya Hussain, a celebrity baker, found it good for her anxiety. It forced you to concentrate on the job in hand and clear your thoughts for a while.

Although lockdown had eased my anxiety and allowed me to get my thoughts and plans together I was acutely aware of close friends of mine who were now under financial stress. The world needed to get back to some normality for them and I may have to step back on my hamster wheel, but I had put a stick in the side of it to slow it down. This is what I wrote in my notebook before lockdown: 'It amazes me how ridiculous the world is becoming. Walking to the hospital I saw cars passing me. Everyone was in their own little world. No one seems particularly happy. People were working all hours because everything costs so much'.

It is ironic that I had mentioned pandemics in my last book. My initial fear has subsided partly because I thought I may have already had it and partly because we were being careful. There had been some uplifting stories in lockdown, for example:

1) Covid survival stories of a premature baby the size my son was when he was born and people over 100 years old.

2) Captain Tom becoming an Honorary Colonel and being knighted by the Queen.

3) A double rainbow being spotted on NHS clapping night.

4) Increased family time (e.g., all getting to see the International Space Station as it passed over our conservatory).

Even I, a 'seasoned lockdown personality', one who used to impose the odd lockdown at the weekend because I couldn't cope with everyday life, would sometimes get frustrated or concerned about the effects of it all on my mental health. I would decide to take my car for a quick spin knowing it wouldn't do it any good stuck in the garage. I would drive it to somewhere quiet for exercise. Not the beaches as they had become busy again. I realised if I left it too long my confidence in driving would be affected and I may become institutionalised.

Last year I had found it difficult leaving hospital even after just four days. I remember the strangest feeling had come over me when I was waiting in the car park with my sons for my husband to collect the car. People were going to need time to adjust. I had recently had a Zoom meeting with three close friends. It had started off quite formal and then after getting booted out of Zoom twice we went onto Messenger and it all turned into a fun party with each of us using effects such as making ourselves princesses or unicorns or monsters. My particular favourite was being a spaceman. It emphasised how much I liked my current bubble even if I did look like a chipmunk in it!

I had initially been quite frightened about the virus and even worried about touching the bins after the binmen. It had been mentioned that the news had heightened people's anxiety but some was necessary for people to take Covid seriously. In the early days I had heard of my childhood doctor dying and the shocking news that the mum of one of our students had passed away from the virus. On the news it had mentioned people being arrested after licking their hands and then touching food in a supermarket. This behaviour had understandably made many people angry. People had also been coughed on in a threatening way.

The world did seem to be in turmoil at the moment. All the tensions in Hong Kong and now talk of a possible Cold War between China and America. Tensions in the UK government had seemed particularly high this year, stemming from the handling of Brexit.

I had come up with a new slogan:

Avoid people: Avoid Stress: But don't forget Happiness

I don't necessarily mean become a hermit but be quite selective about the people and the number of people around you. Avoid stress – I was quite good at this. I think sometimes I came across as 'lazy' but it was kind of a self-protection mechanism. Do what makes you and others happy and with parenting I was learning to move from protection mode to help mode. I had, since my last book, started to live again and I was recognising any difficulties I was still facing and tackling them when I wanted to.

Things had recently started to come together despite being told that I would be redundant. I had been determined to carry on helping in a school so I had got a place on the Academic Mentoring scheme. Ironically I had asked Boris Johnson for a similar role months ago on Twitter! I had heard nothing back. I guess if you want something you've got to decide what it is and 'go out and get it'.

I hadn't gone out but I had completed a strenuous Zoom interview and many forms. Progress was also being made on some of my fears. I had been forced to use the big car down some narrow lanes to pick up my husband after he came off his bike and broke his finger and damaged the rotator cuff of his elbow. I just got on with it, probably because I didn't have time to worry about it.

My Parkinson's medicine seemed to be working well and I was less shaky and I was experiencing less apathy. Things were getting sorted at home partly due to lockdown and it looked like I could get that part-time job that I had hoped for even if it was initially only for one year. I was going to be in a school helping where it was needed – to support students who had fallen behind due to Covid. In the meantime online tutoring was great and it kept me on my toes.

In my last book I had touched on some of the challenging behaviour in schools. I had more training during lockdown on attachment and this had explained how childhood stress could cause such behaviours. I had a new understanding of how background, which was no fault of the child or on my part, could produce a vicious cycle. Stress really had a lot to answer for and stress could be passed on so easily. Stress was a contagion in its own right and it was a hidden pandemic.

Looking through my journal I saw notes about some of the negative behaviours I had seen since my last book. Reading them now no longer made me anxious, it was like the extended time away from school had allowed me to detach from it. Clearly short weekends had not been enough in the past. One incident note made me smile, it was about icing sugar being thrown around as it had accidently been left in a classroom. It had all been logged on the behaviour system. I could hear different teachers and the technician blaming themselves for leaving it out, but surely teenagers should show some self-control. In the end no harm had been done but extra cleaning was required. I'm not saying behaviour problems have gone away because they never will, but things were going in the right direction. Staff numbers were stabilising, it seemed, and behaviour systems in the school were clearer.

I feel some of life is down to fate and some of it is down to what you make of it. My place on the Academic Mentoring Programme had come about because I had picked up a bookmark with a website leading to it. My choice of husband had been partly down to me drinking punch before a night out at university. My choice of university had been down to picking up a prospectus from a pile in a room at school. They didn't really do career advice then. The rest had been filled in by hard work, some wrong and right decisions, and a bit of luck. Follow your individual path as best you can and don't spend so much time worrying that you are missing good times.

A good illustration of how worry can make things go wrong was when I recently made my dad's 75th birthday cake. At the end of lockdown I had made a near perfect lemon meringue cake. He had commented on how good it was so I set my heart on recreating it. The day before he was due round I started to feel the pressure and we over-mixed it resulting in a collapsed cake. Thankfully the second cake was better, although it still wasn't as good as the first (it hadn't risen as much and was a little drier). The meringue was awesome though. The fun had gone out of making it to a certain extent because I had compared it to the earlier one and put myself under pressure.

I had also learned that a job gave you identity but it could take so much more if you weren't careful. I had come up with another thought to end this book but I hadn't written it in my notepad. I remembered it in bed but then promptly forgot it in the morning… anyway not to worry. Again I will end on a happy note. One of my happiest nights happened this year. We had made it out to Corfu for a week during the pandemic and we were on our penultimate night. That day we had been to Kassiopi and snorkelled and had great food.

It was so picturesque. We had achieved so much as a family that holiday (and in general). Like life there had been some stressful moments as the roads were 'hairy' and coaches would appear out of nowhere but there had been some great moments too. The next day would be a relaxation day...

Further Information

Voice for Anxiety series so far:

1) The Sapphire Conspiracy and beyond it all
2) Moving Away From Anxiety and Writing Out My Bread Crumb List
Also see Voice for Anxiety (book) on Facebook for information and discussions on anxiety.

References

1) https://arstechnica.com/science/2010/11/why-neurons-die-in-parkinsons-patients/

2) https://www.calmclinic.com/anxiety/causes/serotonin-deficiency

3) https://www.calmclinic.com/anxiety/symptoms/low-blood-pressure

4) https://www.frontiersin.org/articles/10.3389/fnana.2015.00091/full

5) https://www.independent.co.uk/life-style/health-and-families/alcohol-stress-coping-mechanism-uk-adults-drinking-wine-beer-a8159721.html.

6) https://healthfully.com/434221-dark-chocolate-and-serotonin.html

7) https://www.michaeljfox.org/symptoms?smcid=ag-a1b1R0000086fMw

8) https://www.nature.com/collections/ypjcncrzxn (images Google)
Credit: Philip Patenall/Macmillan Publishers Limited[8]

9) https://www.nhs.uk/conditions/psychosis/causes/

10) https://www.ninds.nih.gov/News-Events/News-and-Press-Releases/Press-Releases/toxic-form-dopamine-may-stress-out-brain-cells

11) https://parkinsonsnewstoday.com/approved-treatments/azilect-rasagiline/

12) https://parkinsonsnewstoday.com/2017/06/29/3-things-can-cause-psychosis-parkinsons-disease/

13) https://www.parkinsons.org.uk/information-and-support/anxiety

14) Parkinson's treatment: The 10 Secrets to a Happier Life,

Michael S. Okun, M.D. English Version, 2013, p83.

15)
https://www.recoveryformula.com/quiz/start?utm_expid=.
soruMCiNTp68LVKt_9_htA.0&utm_referrer=
16) https://www.scientificamerican.com/article/the-science-behind-dreaming/
17)   https://www.thebestbrainpossible.com/why-you-need-to-give-your-brain-a-break/
18)   http://www.yalescientific.org/2011/11/aromatherapy-exploring-olfaction/

Printed in Great Britain
by Amazon